Reminiscences Of Childhood At Inverkeithing, Or Life At A Lazaretto

LAZARETTO, INVERKEITHING BAY, FIFESHIRE (1829.)

REMINISCENCES

OF

CHILDHOOD AT INVERKEITHING,

OR

LIFE AT A LAZARETTO.

BY

JAMES SIMSON,

Editor of

"SIMSON'S HISTORY OF THE GIPSIES,"

and Author of

"CONTRIBUTIONS TO NATURAL HISTORY AND PAPERS ON OTHER SUBJECTS";
"CHARLES WATERTON"; "THE ENGLISH UNIVERSITIES AND JOHN
BUNYAN"; AND "THE SCOTTISH CHURCHES AND THE GIPSIES."

" . . . . . . O! is all forgot?
All school-days' friendship, childhood innocence?"—SHAKSPEARE.

NEW YORK: JAMES MILLER.
EDINBURGH: MACLACHLAN & STEWART.
LONDON: BAILLIÈRE, TYNDALL & CO.
1882.

PREFACE.

It is seldom in good taste for a person to speak of himself; on which account (and also because there was hardly occasion for it), I avoided doing it in the little I have hitherto published. The present Reminiscences, I trust, will prove one of the exceptions, for the following reasons, among others :—1st, they refer exclusively up to the time when I lacked three or four months of being ten years of age; 2d, it is upwards of thirty years since I left Scotland; and 3d, three thousand miles separate me from the places alluded to: all of which circumstances, if they do not disarm ungenerous criticism, at least satisfy me in regard to what might otherwise be questionable, if not offensive, even to myself.

My connection with authorship proceeded incidentally from having come into possession of a MS. on the Gipsies, left by my father, who collected the matter of it, at the urgent request of Sir Walter Scott and William Blackwood, mainly between 1817 and 1831,* while residing at the Lazaretto; and in regard to which, Sir Walter Scott, in a note to *Quentin Durward* (1831), said that "it is to be hoped this gentleman will publish the knowledge he possesses on so singular a topic." And it is partly in relation to this work that I have prepared these Reminiscences, as alluded to in the Appendix. It was also with this object in view that I published *Contributions to Natural History and Papers on Other Subjects*; so that what I wrote in *The Scottish Churches and the Gipsies* was strictly true :—" As regards myself, I am so incidentally connected with authorship as not to own it, except to a very few personal friends; to withhold a knowledge of it from whom would be almost equivalent to denying it " (p. 15).

In the Preface to *Contributions, etc.*, I said :—" I would have added to them but for the difficulty in finding subjects (or leisure to develop them), that have not been treated before, or treated in such a way as to require to be corrected, and placed on another and more permanent foundation than heretofore." This remark does not very inaptly apply to the present publication, for the reminiscences of a person under ten years of age—whatever they might be—cannot but be more or less interesting, provided that they are minute, circumstantial, and accurate; in all of which re-

---

* " History of the Gipsies," p. 64.—I brought the work down to the date of publication.

spects they will speak for themselves. It makes little difference if they are given from memory many years afterwards.

A publication like this, so far from being common, is hardly conventional; for which reason it may be objected to; but, on the other hand, it may be taken as a precedent that will lead to others of the same kind.

It has often been asked, At what age is a child, at least in a general way, responsible? As regards myself, I do not remember when I did not consider myself responsible; and I have no recollection of having pleaded the "Baby Act" on any occasion. The development of a human being from childhood to mature age, however interesting, is foreign to this work, except that it may be said that he is only a "child of a larger growth," whose relation to a parent proper never ceases. Some people have little definite recollection of their existence while under ten years of age, and not much more of their boyhood. My removal from the neighbourhood of the scenes depicted had the effect of leading me to look back on them, and having them indelibly impressed on my memory. To such as remember the events of their childhood, in a semi-rural place, what I have told of mine will doubtless prove attractive; whatever may be said of purely town-brought-up people, or such as, "caring for none of these things," are for the most part engrossed in their callings, and the amenities connected with their positions in life. It is astonishing how deficient many seem to be in the mental flexibility that enables others to look back and forward, and throw themselves into positions besides those they had been long and carefully trained to fill.

Humanity is so uniform in the principles of its physical and moral and even its social nature that a description of it, in its leading features, might serve for one age as well as another; and generation has succeeded generation almost as if they had never been, except that latterly each has left little more than "stray notices" of its existence, that are not always reliable. In that respect, is it not possible that the descriptions of the places given in the Reminiscences can be preserved, where there would otherwise have been a blank?

In childhood a person is in many ways greatly indebted to others; but allowing for that, it may be said that in his "controversies" with his fellow-creatures the principal means that are necessary to his ends are his tongue and fists, and his legs when things come to the worst: how different from the complicated relationship in which he stands in that respect to them in after-life!

New York, *4th January,* 1882.

REMINISCENCES

OF

CHILDHOOD AT INVERKEITHING.

O N the southern side of the narrow entrance to the inner bay or harbour of Inverkeithing — commonly called the West Ness—stood a Lazaretto, which was finally discontinued as a Government quarantine establishment in the autumn of 1835, when it was sold to an Edinburgh lawyer for £200, but burdened with an annual feu duty of £20. It comprised a wooden and a stone building, inside of a stone wall probably twenty feet high at some parts of it, and a dwelling-house, close to the west side, in which I was born on the 4th of January, 1826.

After leaving the place in September or October, 1835, I was told by one of the old boatmen that, before this establishment was erected, a ship laid alongside of the pier, sunk into the sand by stone, and served the purpose of a Lazaretto; and that when the Lazaretto proper was built this stone was partly used for building dry dykes, while the rest was thrown into the sea, on the east side of the wall mentioned; which latter information satisfied a curiosity that I always had as to the meaning of the stone being there. I was also told that this ship, on being taken to Leith, was lost on the sands a little to the west of Cramond island.

The Lazaretto was three stories high, and was built throughout of the best Memel timber. It was placed upon a number of square stone supports, some of which were continued inside of the building to the beginning of the roof, to steady the structure. The stone used inside appeared to be of a soft and inferior quality, yet doubtless suitable for its purpose, as it was not exposed to the weather; but for about three feet from the ground on the outside it was of a harder and better description. The building had thus an almost clear open space under it, sufficiently high to allow a child to move about by slightly stooping. Its three floors were not solid, for between each plank was space sufficient to admit the shoe of a child, who had to be careful in walking that its feet were not caught in the intervals. The sides and ends of the building were composed of a frame, and slats that opened and shut laterally; so that the structure could be thoroughly ventilated from below and all around, and have its contents exposed to the air outside. The size of the building was that of the machine shop of Mr. Scott, erected some time after 1835, for I was told that its roof was the identical one that covered the Lazaretto.

The only use that I can recollect the Lazaretto being put to was to receive a quantity of what I afterwards understood to be bags of rags, which were landed at the pier from lighters, and I believe broken up and ventilated, to remove the contagion which they were supposed to contain. The stone building, back of the wooden one, was apparently intended for passengers; but it was never used, within my recollection, for any purpose but housing the labourers; and its only furniture consisted of the slats of three beds, built into the walls of the room in which they slept. There was a rigid quarantine observed. The food of the men was passed in through an aperture in the wall, on what looked like the half of a barrel cut lengthwise, with shelves, on which the food was placed; and this on being turned on a pivot reached the inside, when the outside door was locked. Water was poured into a chamber attached to the large door, and caught from a pipe inside. Coals were shovelled, almost thrown, through a door—no one being allowed to approach within a certain distance on either side. The wall had two doors; a small one for passengers, and a large one to admit merchandise on hand trucks, along a flagged way from the pier till it reached hoisting apparatus connected with the building. About half a dozen steps led to the building itself, and three or four led from it to the stone building behind it. In the S. E. corner of the enclosure was a small, dilapidated stone building that apparently had been used as a temporary smithy; and near the N. E. corner was a small wooden erection attached to the back of the superintendent's office and boatmen's watch-house, which were entered from the outside of the wall. Attached to the entrance to the wooden building, on either side of it, was a shed built of stone. Inside of the stone wall were various trees which I need not describe.

At this time there were five or six hulks, mostly ships of the line dismantled, anchored in St. Margaret's Hope, a little below Limekilns, that were also used for quarantine purposes. The *Dartmouth*, a large-sized frigate, which formed part of the fleet commanded by Lord Exmouth in his attack on Algiers, remained, for years afterwards, the only hulk. The rest disappeared under circumstances unknown to me, excepting the last of them, which I remember seeing, in tow of a steamer, passing Barnbougle Point, as I stood on the highest part of the garden of the school-teacher, in the summer of 1835; and I could not help contrasting the wonderful difference between a large ship of war when full rigged and when used as a hulk.

The Lazaretto had been practically discontinued for some time before I remember it, for I recollect my mother saying that she had lost a large bag of feathers which she had omitted to remove out of it when the labourers entered it during the cholera, in 1832. My father let his house outside, for one season, at least, to Mr. Elias Cathcart of Auchendraine, Ayrshire, for sea-bathing, and removed with his family to the house inside the wall. It was his wife who made the pencil drawing of the place from a photograph of which the frontispiece has been prepared. In 1835 the trees in front of the dwelling-house, when viewed from the East Ness, covered everything but the chimney tops; and the drawing having been made from the same place, it would appear that the view was taken about 1829.

The first recollection of people must necessarily be connected with something outside of the daily routine of their existence, and that presents salient points. Thus I recollect being lifted into a large boat of a light, tar-like colour, that was hauled up to the beach at the west side of the pier; and that is all I remember of it. From this I conclude that my memory does not extend beyond that. The next occasion was finding myself in the kitchen of the old farm-house — or rather row of one-storied houses—at the Cruicks, without knowing how I got there, or how I left it; and being gently and kindly shaken by a strange woman inside, who said, "Fat the de'il's the matter wi' the bairn?" This was Nell, wife of Charlie, a stonemason.

I have no recollection of the building of the new steading of the Cruicks, although it was doubtless put up between 1830 and 1831, at the time I made Nell's acquaintance, when she had charge of the old steading. But I have a very distinct remembrance of the building of the new dwelling-house, by seeing two or three masons working at the top of the south side of it, and two labourers carrying stone up to them, as I was with a boy while herding a cow a little to the east of the building. This is all I recollect of the erection of the new buildings at the Cruicks. All of the trees were planted within my remembrance. I recollect when I first went to a tailor at Limekilns, about four miles from our house, walking both ways, and seeing a man sitting on the floor of a room, with some clippings of red cloth lying in a corner, as if they had been rags. I doubtless set out and returned with the greatest ardour, for next morning I could not move one foot after another; and was lifted and placed on a table in the middle of the sitting-room. I can fix my first certain recollection to the 20th of June, 1831, the day before the birth of the fourth boy of the family; for on that day I had Jock Hadden carrying a small Russian mat to the top of a brae and pulling me down on it, and digging and eating earth-nuts. The next day the most of the children had the same mat a short distance behind our house, with a stoup, painted blue, with black-coloured hoops, containing water, with a tin to drink it out of, and oatmeal cakes to eat. It was a beautiful day, and early in the afternoon we were told of the birth, and asked to go into the house and see the "little Irishman."

Nell, whom I have mentioned, had also charge of the new Cruicks' steading. She was an Aberdeen woman, whom we all liked, although I could never get rid of the idea that her eye was constantly on me when on or about the premises. She had small and *girning* features, and was anything but good-looking; and was of a nervous and fussing disposition, constantly indulging in such expressions as "Fat the de'il is this?" or "Fat the de'il is that?" She had no children. Her husband was a remarkably big and fat and gruff-looking, but peaceable man, and a wonderful eater. To us children he looked like an ogre, that could dispose of a pail of milk and a pound of butter, not counting eggs, at a meal. And the owner of the farm, who was a non-resident, had evidently misgivings on that head, for it was generally reported and believed that he had said, "What a pity it was that the cholera did not carry off muckle Charlie!" There was doubtless some truth in this; at least he was of a very *careful* disposition, for I heard a friend of his, after visiting him at the farm, when he took up his residence on it, say, "——'s mice might break their necks, but would not burst themselves." It was also said that the size of some of the windows of his house arose from his having bought the sashes at a bargain, and built to suit them.

The farm-house mentioned stood about a third of a mile from the Lazaretto, which was built on ground cultivated by a farmer resident in Inverkeithing, there being no buildings on it. About half the land was arable and the rest not broken up.

It would seem that employment under the Government creates not only a class, but almost a caste in a small community. As children we all felt that there was a distinction of some kind, although we could not understand the cause or meaning of it. It being the quarantine station, distant about a mile from a community of about 1,700 people, and our father being the superintendent, and what may be generally described as a thoroughly respectable character, the people treated us all with not only courtesy, but kindness. On that head I never had occasion to feel otherwise than pleased. If I had any trouble, it proceeded either from some fault of my own or from what will affect children under almost any circumstances. With the exception of two families, the heads of which were employed at the station, we were the only residents on the ground on part of which, or near which, the Lazaretto stood ; and, although we had no right to order any one off, we felt (unreasonably, perhaps,) that people had no business there, excepting those that cultivated the ground or came to visit us. We could not order them off, but we made it very manifest that they were not wanted there, especially boys or half-grown lads. Thus my father would make as though he was watching them, and disappear and then appear, which had an ominous meaning, and generally served the purpose in view. One Sunday, rather early, there appeared about half a dozen of what looked like young men, one of whom I knew ; and my father cast a peculiar glance at them, which I instantly appreciated, for I joined in the crowd till I saw them beyond the boundary. On one occasion I and my sister next older than me saw a strange boy with the farmer's herd, and we went to see who he was. His head was bare and had so peculiar an appearance that we, Scotch - like, instantly dubbed him "Tappie - tourie" ; and I had to stand between him and my sister to preserve the peace, for she looked as if she would instantly fly at him. However, the herd's acquaintances were always privileged when we ascertained that they were really such. An old man, poorly dressed and very miserable-looking, -once caused us no little fear. He hung around the place daily for nearly a week, with no apparent means of feeding or sleeping ; and it was the daily enquiry of my father on coming

home, about four o'clock, if "the old fellow had left." No concern was felt at night, but only during the day in my father's absence. He even attempted to scrape acquaintance with my mother, and asked her if she kept a school—there being eight of us ; when she, rather cautiously, said, "Yes, she kept a kind of a school." However, the "old fellow" attempted to drown himself, but changed his mind when in the water, and disappeared, to our great relief. For the reasons given, everything became so quiet that even the cow would approach a stranger with surprise and without fear ; which once led to a ludicrous scene. My father heard Crummie making a strange and loud noise, and on going to ascertain the cause of it, found her *tearing* in the direction of the house with a man holding on to her tail. He instantly let go his hold of it, and said that he was a sailor that had had experience in the East Indies with wild cattle, and that his safety when attacked by them depended on his catching them by the tail and holding on to it, whatever might happen. It turned out that the cow had gone up to him in the most friendly manner, which Jack construed into a challenge ; hence the result. The poor animal when freed instantly turned round and stared at him.

There was no road to the Lazaretto, except a foot-path for only part of the way ; for the rest was over the beach that was covered at high tide, so that a detour had sometimes to be made in going to and from it. In some places only there would be the remains of the ruts made by cart wheels when one happened to go in that direction. The inner bay or harbour became dry at low water, so that my father, when in a hurry to reach the town of Inverkeithing in the morning, would cross to the East Ness on stilts to keep his feet dry when passing the shallow channel ; and return in the same direction in the afternoon, by calling on one of the boatmen to go over and ferry him and his stilts to where he had started from. In this way he would cut off fully three-fourths of the distance to St. Davids.

The only people that lived near the Lazaretto were two families. The first consisted of Daniel Nicol and his wife, and a young woman related in some way to them. Daniel ceased to be employed in the establishment after the cholera in 1832. He seemed to have owned his house, which was next to ours, with a hedge between them; and to have built the other three sides of his garden fence, from the stone ballast that was discharged from the old *floating* Lazaretto. He appears to have been originally a gardener, or a farm servant, or one that understood gardening thoroughly, for he kept the ground well cultivated. It contained a fine variety of gooseberries and currants of every kind; none of which he ever sold or gave away, nor could the inmates of his house possibly use more than a small part of what was grown. We had nothing of the kind on our side of the hedge, or inside of the quarantine wall. Close to the drystone fences of Daniel's garden were currants in the greatest quantity; and sometimes he would tell us to help ourselves *over* the fence, and sometimes let us do it without telling us. At other times he would make a dreadful noise if he saw us even touch a berry. This was a great temptation to so many children; and as they could not understand the singular caprice of the man, they came to the conclusion that they had almost a right to help themselves whether they were told to do it or not. After leaving the employment in the Lazaretto, I do not know how Daniel lived. He kept a cow, and he must have had some little money; for one day in passing at some distance from his door my sister next older to me picked up a pound, in my presence, which my mother sent to him, not doubting that it was his, when he raised a great disturbance, by saying that the child stole it out of his house. He was considered an "ill-haired auld loon," whose nose always fell a-bleeding on my mother alluding to a large bag of feathers which she had omitted to remove from the Lazaretto on its being occupied in consequence of the cholera, as I have already mentioned. None of us liked him, and I the least of any, particularly after his threatening to send me to Dunfermline jail under the following circumstances:—

There was a small flock of sheep pastured in the autumn on the land back of the Lazaretto, with which he had nothing to do. I was in the habit of going at night and catching one of the sheep and riding it; and I got so fond of the sport that I would do it in the day-time, by driving the sheep where they could not be seen. I succeeded, towards the evening, in catching the biggest sheep of the flock, and got on its back, and felt absolutely happy, when a terrible "hollo" from behind made me tumble off the sheep's back, without daring to look around to see who the person was, or what he wanted. Then I heard Daniel's gruff voice saying, "Get up and be ready to go to Dunfermline jail with me to-morrow morning, immediately after breakfast." My happiness was soon changed into misery, for I really believed that that would happen which was threatened.

Much as I disliked Daniel personally, I had a heart's hatred for his cat; and it was difficult to separate the two in my mind. I seldom saw it, and never could approach it. Daniel had evidently been settled there from the time that the land was wild, for his wife used to say that adders or vipers were so common that they would seem to move about among her feet as she would hoe her potatoes. His breed of cats seemed to have grown so wild as little more than nominally to admit of domesticated relations. Inside of the high wall of the quarantine I let my rabbits run at large; their only covering from wet being the wooden building and sheds before alluded to. Every young rabbit, whether tame or wild, put into the enclosure disappeared, nor could a brood be reared; the old rabbits only held their own. I was satisfied that there were no weasels or rats inside of the wall, and I could refer the mischief only to Daniel's cat; and my only remedy was to get my father to line the trunk of a tree (the branches of which nearly touched the wall) with dry whin bushes, but without effect. For the cat evidently climbed to the top of the wall on the S. W. corner, where it was not far from the ground on the outside, as compared with the height within.

Daniel's wife, a tottering old woman, very well liked by us, went under no other name than "Auld Luck." Almost as far back as I can recollect, I remember her getting a cow, and engaging for her herd Jock Hadden, the youngest son of Mark Hadden, one of the quarantine boatmen; and asking him to go into her house to get his "arles" (what bind a bargain). Feeling curious to know what was meant by Jock getting his "arles," I followed, and saw her with her thumb spread a large oatmeal cake with butter, which Jock ate with great relish. I have said that we were not particular about helping ourselves to currants *over* the stone fence of Daniel's garden; but I once ventured inside of it for that purpose, when "Auld Luck" made her appearance. I immediately crawled between some pease that were high in their growth, and well sticked up, and fit for picking; when the tottering old body began to pick them right over me. I naturally felt uncomfortable, but less so when I quietly turned round face upwards, and fixed my eyes on her countenance and perceived that she did not notice me.

The young woman spoken of was Lizzie Nicol, generally called "Pussie Nicol." She was regarded by us with the greatest affection, and we were hardly ever separated from her. I have said that she was in some way related to old Daniel and his wife; but she seemed much superior to them, allowing for the difference in their ages. She was a tall and rather slim but handsome young woman, with dark brown hair, pretty blue eyes, and florid complexion; and was almost lady-like in her bearing, so far as a child could judge. She was frequently dressed in a blue gown with small white spots, which took with us all. All, besides the children, liked her. I well remember the piteous feeling which she showed on finding that on putting my brother next youngest to me down from her arms, his cheek almost became ript open by a needle that was in her bosom. She left the place before us. The last I remember of her was her racing Daniel's cow backwards and forwards, as fast as it could run, while my father dashed a pail of water over it each time, to cure it of the effects of having eaten too freely of wet clover. Whatever became of her, she remained embalmed in our memories.

The other family consisted of Mark Hadden, the boatman, his wife, and three sons and two daughters. There was nothing particular about Mark except that he was lazy and uncouth-looking, and somewhat bent in his person, and blind of an eye, or had something the matter with it. On one Sunday morning, pretty early for a Sunday, I saw his wife treating him, while sitting between the fire and the window, as children are generally treated once a week, when if the labour is not more or less successful, they are hardly considered healthy; but I never saw a man so treated before. I reported what I saw to my mother, as something like "black cattle in a park." The "planting of the thorn" was a more agreeable scene, for we all turned out, under the most pleasant circumstances, to carefully prepare the ground and plant a small hawthorn tree, with every demonstration of success to it; and which we often visited and tended with care. I cannot say the same of the killing of Mark's pig, for it happened when I was almost ready to start for school; but do what I could, and short as the distance was, I arrived only after the family had got the liver put into the frying-pan for breakfast. I felt shocked by the haste shown on the occasion.

Mrs. Hadden, generally called "Luckie Hadden," accused me once of theft under the following circumstances :—On my way to school, and immediately to the west of her house, but *outside* of her premises, my eye suddenly caught sight of a round and clearly defined hole of moderate size that led into a whin bush, as it touched and became mixed with the grass. The conclusion was unavoidable that there was something peculiar there, so that I put in my arm and brought out a soda water bottle (the first I ever saw) more than half full. On finding that it contained whiskey, I instantly took it to a rock on the beach and smashed it into many pieces. I had no proof as to whose whiskey it was, but no doubt that it belonged to Luckie Hadden, who was a drunken old jade. After performing what I considered a good deed, I had no other thoughts than that of telling my mother, when I returned from school, what I had done, and of passing Hadden's house in my usual manner. None of its inmates had proof that I had even seen the whiskey, but they entertained no doubt as to the offender; and all of them—parents as well as children—were on the watch for me, and abused me sadly, calling me by every name they could lay their tongues on. And "steal the whiskey" stuck to me for many days; but I neither admitted nor denied it. It was doubtless a heart-breaking disappointment to the poor woman when she missed her bottle; but she should have been more careful in hiding it, and not have tempted a child to do what it did.

I have already spoken of Jock Hadden as Mrs. Nicol's herd. He is the first person I remember of that stirred in my breast the feeling of anger. He had promised me a stick with a peculiarly crooked head and did not give it to me. With this exception, I was very partial to Jock, and he was very kind to me. He had a great knack for building children's houses; and I remember how happy I felt when we shared between us one that contained a chimney of brick, neatly plastered, so far as a child of that age could judge.—Annie Hadden was lame, and looked as if palsied on one side, and mentally deficient, and wore boots for her deformed limb. Still, she was a resource when I happened to fall out with my three sisters, all older than myself; on which occasions they would reproach me with, "Gang wi' Annie Hadden, gang wi' Annie Hadden!" and once they managed to strike up some doggerel in connection with us. But these separations did not last long.

Our next neighbours were an old blacksmith, his wife, and his daughter Rachel, or "Rech," that married the foreman of the Cruicks' farm, who bore a Highland name. Their house stood on the left on leaving the Inverkeithing road to go to the Ferry by the old way over the hills. The old blacksmith was a queer-looking little creature, but very entertaining; and his wife was an "old crow" that was seldom seen. "Rech" was a country lass, of a huthery-tuthery make-up, and black-eyed, and by no means ill-looking. She was partial to us children, and we rather liked her. But sometimes there would be dis-satisfaction felt on our receiving articles that were left at her father's house for us to call or send for them. The smithy, as is the case in country places, was a general resort for certain kinds of people ; and I would frequently go there to see the blacksmith's monkey, (the first one I ever saw), and his bull-terrier " Pincher," which would follow me, and " take the water " as well as any water-dog proper. " Rech's " husband would spruce himself up of a Sunday, and set out to church in his blue coat with brass buttons, as big as anybody ; but there was a sad comedown when I met him some years afterwards in Leith, picking up stray work as a porter.

The people mentioned were the only inhabitants on the north side of the peninsula, living within a mile of us, and whose dwellings were within sight of Inverkeithing. The other inhabitants lived on the coast or shore on the south side, and consisted of the toll-keeper, Mr. Cathcart (already alluded to), whose property of St. Margaret's Point long afterwards became Captain Elder's, Mr. Pringle of the Ferry Barns, and the residents at and immediately above the Ferry.

At the time to which I allude the chemical works (afterwards called Jamestown) had been out of use for some time, and were closed. I remember when they were in operation, and of seeing magnesia made, immediately to the left of the entrance; and an old man driving two carts of coals to the works daily. The last season I saw Ord, the celebrated circus-rider, perform was in a turf ring in front of the building, where the road strikes off for the Ness, when he retired to the gate of it (which was closed) to change his apparel to suit his characters. On the time previous to that he entered inside of the gate for the same purpose. His only remuneration was a lottery ; I think a sixpence a chance. A wealthy man living in the neighbourhood won a boll of oatmeal, and the buzz of the assemblage was, "Now the poor will be considered"; but the worthy man said that the meal was for his own poor, that is, his own family.

The old Cruicks' farm-houses were not used after the new steading was built, except for occasional purposes, such as holding harvest-homes, or "kirns" as they were called. I recollect having missed being present at one of these, and of examining the place with the herd the next morning. He caught a large mouse and flayed it, spreading its fat over it as we see done with a lamb, and expressed his wonder at how it had feasted the night before. "No, no," said I, "that mouse did not take on that fat in one night."

In the summer of 1834 a boy from one of the grocers in Inverkeithing brought to our house a large English cheese and several bottles of brandy, which our mother, after considerable question and hesitation, took in, as the boy asserted positively that they were for her. She had the cheese scraped, as it might after all be for her, but she doubted that the brandy was ; that being a thing not used in the house, although there might have been a little kept for medicinal purposes. Whiskey and port and sherry constituted the only liquors ; and these were never used except on conventional occasions. Indeed the only spirit that was in demand was Riga balsam, for cuts, bruises, and what not. It turned out that the cheese and brandy were intended for a family that had taken, as summer quarters, the Cruicks' new farmhouse, which had never been occupied by its owner. This was a temporary addition to the inhabitants of a different order from what we were accustomed to. The head of the house, a tall, well-built, well-filled-up, fair and florid, and fine-looking man, that rode a large and handsome horse, and his son, equally prepossessing, mounted on a fine Shetland pony, were what we had never seen before. An intimate acquaintance instantly sprang up. The son was too much of a man in importance to keep company with the like of us ; but his sister, accompanied by a pretty little black and white spaniel, went with my three sisters and myself to see what sights children have to show on such occasions. First we showed her the Ferry Hills, east of the road, clothed throughout in the finest of pasture, and (one might say) covered with horses, cattle and sheep ; then the various scenes in all directions ; and after that Port Laing sands, the salmon stake-nets there, and the place where some snow was always found after it had disappeared everywhere else, in consequence of it slipping off the hill and accumulating in the hollow below. Previously none of us had ever thought of passing over the pasture land, where there were so many horses and cattle, unless we were with a grown-up person; but the sheep we were never afraid of, although sometimes a little suspicious of the rams. We sat down on the edge of the land at Port Laing, safe from possible danger, and discussed the subject of its occupants, especially the "dreadful bulls" that might be there. The pretty little spaniel, anything like which I had never seen before, attracted my attention far more than its mistress, interesting as she was, and a city girl at that ; and we were playing at her back when she suddenly exclaimed : —"Oh, dear, what will Papa and Mamma say when they find that Neppie has been worrying all the sheep ? Neppie, Neppie, where's Neppie ?" On hearing his name called, Neppie ran to her, and was covered with reproaches and caresses for the fright he had given her, although he could not have stood up to one sheep if she had had a lamb by her side.

We then started for our house, to show the Lazaretto, and opposite to it St. Davids, the wooded hill, the flag-staff, the East Ness, and Inverkeithing stretching to the westward, and the bay, which had a pretty appearance at high tide. In our way we took in what little things children, so isolated as us, are apt to designate by a name—the wash-bowl, the castle, the coach, the cradle, our uncle's ship, and such objects as others would not notice, or attach any meaning to. The wash-bowl was a rock having a hollow on the top that was filled at the highest tides, or when the waves rose, or by rain. Our newly-made acquaintance would wash her hands and face in the bowl, after which I made an insinuation as to its contents, which greatly distressed her ; but I soothed her by protesting that it really was not so. We then came to the castle, and were proceeding to the next object when, to my astonishment, our friend and my second sister began a fight which ended in a "rough and tumble." At this time I was familiar with cock-fights, dog-fights and boy-fights, and had fought some battles myself. The quarrels of girls which I had seen had been confined to calling names, sometimes spitting at each other, and at the worst pulling caps ; but here was a real fight. The old idea at once seized me to see fair-play, whatever the result ; but when I saw the two girls tumbling over each other, almost like dogs, and the stranger uppermost, I at once pulled her off. It was always a mystery to me why the girls, who were aged nearly 13, fell out in such a way, as their dispositions were the very opposite of being quarrelsome. The most striking thing about the matter was, that after being separated everything became as pleasant between them as before ; and we finished the day's excursion as if nothing of the kind had happened.

The intercourse with the family mentioned continued till they left for their home, with nothing but the most agreeable associations, excepting that on at least one occasion the bread at the table turned out to have been borrowed from "that auld craw," the blacksmith's wife.

After this family had left, Mark Hadden's house, the second from ours towards the west, was occupied by one Giles, an Irish marine, and his wife, a little Irish woman. He had lost an arm in the service, and was living on a pension. He was a very tall and fine-looking man, which struck me afterwards when I saw it stated that all the Irish Giles' (in a certain district) were tall men. Living, as it were, on half pay, Giles seemed to take to us as Government people in active service; and became imbued with similar sentiments in regard to outsiders. Even his wife shared the same feeling, and, Irish as she was, she seems to have picked up a Scotch word having a peculiar meaning. Thus, when a strange girl was hanging about her door and staring at the premises, I heard her say, "What do you want here, and what are you glouring at?"

Giles took a fancy to me, and I got on well with him. He particularly asked me to tell him when I saw a frog in his well, which I therefore scrutinized very closely when passing both ways; feeling curious to know what could be his object, as I had always understood that it was desirable to have a frog visit a well. One day I was pleased to find the long-sought-for frog, and I rushed to his house with, "Giles, there's a frog in your well!" In great haste he seized a stick with three prongs in triangular fashion at the end of it and started for the well. He instantly caught the frog on the three-pronged spear and killed it, which did not raise him in my estimation.

He and his wife had a hobby for chickens and reared many of them, having fully a hundred at a time. On coming home, at about one o'clock in the morning, from some special meeting or party in Inverkeithing, my father on passing his place heard a peculiar noise in the hen-house, which he could not reach from where he stood. He listened for a moment and became convinced that there was a person in the house killing the chickens; and, raising a great shout, threatened to blow his brains out. Like one confounded, a man, with as great a shout of fear, started almost from under his feet, and bolted through the hedge of the garden. Several loud knocks brought no response from Giles, but his wife was heard to say, little louder than a whisper and evidently in fear, "Giles, there's something wrong to-night"; and but for which the conclusion would have been that both Giles and his wife were from home. But when he heard a friendly voice calling out, "Get up, Giles, you have lost all your chickens," he was soon on his feet, with a lantern in his hand.

Next morning I was all excitement to be at the scene, where I found a number of chickens going about with their necks more or less bare, showing that the fellow had not been up to his business. I then visited the roost, and looking around discovered that the thief had stood on no ceremony in going, but left a clear gap in the hawthorn hedge (which was pretty tall, but not thick) from the middle of it upwards. Not a hen had been stolen; but of those dead two of the best were sent to us, and the rest were sold. A bag, bearing the marks of the Government hulk that rode at anchor in St. Margaret's Hope, was found. The result to us was the presentation of two fine chickens; and to the robber the loss of his bag, the fright he got, doubtless a scratched face in passing through the hedge, and the chagrin at having been balked of his prey.

Besides looking after his chickens Giles had nothing to do, and so he constantly strolled around the coast, and appropriated everything coming ashore that could not be identified by any one; and anything that was of no use to him, and which would suit me, I got from him. Thus he once gave me a neat little sloop fully rigged, with chain and anchor, which a boy claimed; but the only satisfaction he got was, "Go to Giles; I got it from him." At this time I thoroughly understood the meaning of the word "wrecker," and followed the ways of one on everything that came ashore within the limits. On one occasion, well on in the evening, I noticed, with wide-open eyes, a small two-masted craft coming across the bay from near the foundery, and, wet as it was, and wretchedly as I was shod, I instantly proceeded west to appropriate her when she would come ashore; but to my sorrow I perceived a boy, three or four years older than myself, coming in the opposite direction to recover his boat, that apparently had got away from him when sailing it. He arrived before it came to land, a few feet west of Pinkie well, which deprived me of any possible right, which extended only to a thing that beached. He attended the school that I did, and evidently comprehended the situation. The craft was a very handsome schooner, of rather small size; and I remarked, "Better a small one and a good one," when he looked down to my feet with scorn, and replied, "Yes, better small ones and good ones"—in allusion to my having on a pair of one of my sister's shoes, old ones at that, and far too big for me. I had to swallow the insult, for the boy was far too big for me to tackle; but I kept a record of it, in case I might be able to "pay him off" in some way.

As a "wrecker," I was at first rather jealous of Giles, for he was an intruder, and not in "active service," as we were. But his great kindness, and his giving me what suited me, disarmed me of every feeling of the kind mentioned. Many and many a time have I and my brother next youngest to me run around on the rocks from the Ness to Port Laing sands, to find what had been cast ashore. We would dart our eyes from one rock or spot to another, and cry, "I traps that"; and we always respected what each of us "trapsed." If there was anything

worthy of being picked up, we would return by the rocks and take it home. But it would commonly happen that, although each of us had "trapsed" or chosen even a dozen things apiece, we would return by land; and probably I would start the cry of "a weasel," and we would have a run for home—the distance not being great.

The allusion to my sister's old shoes—which I had on, for some special reason which I do not recollect—reminds me that at our isolated residence it was our custom to have what might be called three suits of clothes; one for church, one for school or everyday conventional occasions, and one for home, which was not worth much. And this rule was observed by my father likewise. I well recollect him following, towards dusk, the reapers (close to our house), behind me, as I was gleaning after them for the benefit of my rabbits and pigeons; and his picking up a straw here and there for amusement. A strange female reaper turned round and asked "who that auld beggar was"; which disconcerted them greatly, and was anything but pleasing to me. It was our custom to give a substantial dinner, of broth and beef, and bread and cheese and whiskey, to the reapers for two days every season; and there was always a bottle for the farmer himself, whenever he was on the ground, which soon became known to those in the house. Sometimes he had real complaints of the children trespassing, where there were no fences, and generally pretended ones; but he was never allowed to get the length of making them, for the kind reception and the whiskey bottle always proved a bar to anything of that nature. If he was seen coming up the walk, the bottle was instantly placed on the table, and met his eye before he could open his mouth.

The cholera season of 1832 is vividly impressed on my memory. For some time before that I had been at the parish school, which was dismissed when the pestilence made its appearance in the town and neighbourhood. I have no recollection of having realized in any form the solemnity connected with this visitation of the angel of death; and I am satisfied that I was incapable of doing it at that age, unless it had been of the death of an inmate of the family, or of one with whom I had stood in close and constant relationship. My associations connected with the cholera are those of the most unalloyed pleasure I ever experienced; the event was the golden age of my existence, the epoch to which I soon began to look back as the dim antiquity of real happiness. There were the dismissal of the school, the beautiful weather, the family all at home, their variety of plays and amusements, the bigger boys of the town sailing and squabbling all over the bay, the burning of tar barrels, and the half-solemn, half-exciting discussions of what to me was incomprehensible. Then there were the bustle about the Lazaretto, which had been disused some time before, the boatmen moving about, the receipt and dispatch of merchandise by vessels, the supplying of the men inside the building with necessaries, and my daily watching all these operations. Then there was my father going about the house several times a day with a saucer (having a piece out of the side of it) containing saltpetre and vinegar, and fumigating everything by stirring the contents with a red-hot poker. Then there was us children taking our meals (not playing with "tea things") inside of the hedge at the bottom of the garden, under the trees, on tablecloths spread on the ground. At this time I got what I thought was a real watch, but what became of it I never knew; and a knife, the edge of which was taken off by one of the boatmen for safety, and which I lost, but afterwards recovered after a lapse of what to a child was an age. The whole scene, as I have said, was to me one of real happiness.

I have also a vivid, but not so minute, recollection of the procession on the passing of the Reform Bill, in 1832, a short time I think before the cholera made its appearance. The people from our direction met back of the road between the "witches' knowe" and the chemical works (now Jamestown) and west of the culvert that receives the water passing between the two hills there. We then proceeded to the main street of the town, where I was taken to form part of a procession of the boys of our school; marching two abreast, with peeled willows in our hands, and having Bobbie —— on my left. What vexed me at first, and detracted from the pleasure of the occasion, was that every boy but myself had white trousers; which doubtless arose from our living "out of town," and not being informed of the programme of the procession. We then went down the harbour wynd; on the corner of the entrance to which I noticed my mother shaking her hand at me, which still further detracted from the pleasure of the occasion, in the uncertainty of its meaning. We continued our march to a hollow behind the flag-staff, near the end of the crescent that leads to the East Ness. There we had speeches and huzzaing, music and drinking, and all kinds of excitement. On returning, the procession, or a large part of the people forming it, proceeded to the residence of a shipper of coals overlooking the harbour—a white-coloured house, apparently plastered or stuccoed—and had a speech from him, frequently interrupted by cheering. And there my recollection of the procession ends, excepting whether it was in passing or repassing (most probably the latter) the only cottage on the crescent that had pillars in front of it, that the crowd cheered its inmate, the toast of the town. On returning home, the first thing I did was to ask my mother why she shook her hand at me, at the top of the wynd ; when she said it was because I was "snifftering" (snuffing up when there is nothing to snuff up), which I softly denied, without thinking how she could either have seen or heard me "snifftering" from the distance at which she was from me.

Soon after the cholera in 1832, the Lazaretto was practically discontinued. When we left it, in 1835, what little ground there was attached to it, or inside of its wall, had been sadly neglected. As I have already said, the building was not used for any purpose for some time before the cholera ; but there seems to have been a company of boatmen attached to the station from the time of its erection, some of whom lived in the watch-house. These had little to do, and some of them seem to have attended to the grounds, as a matter of personal taste and pleasure. I do not remember having seen anything done to beautify the premises, or even affect them in any way. Things were allowed to take care of themselves, while people were kept from injuring them. Perhaps the uncertainty of the continuance of the establishment had this effect. At all events, the only time I saw the ground disturbed was when some potatoes were planted inside of the wall, and some cabbage outside, behind the dwelling - house ; but by whose hand this was done I do not remember. I never saw my father even with a spade in his hand, except when burying an unfortunate hare which I had brought home.

One day he started from the house in the direction of Port Laing sands, with a manure or potato fork in his hand, while I carried a basket. I did not ask him what was his object, although he would doubtless have told me if I had done it. The fork I had often seen, and had once used for a peculiar purpose, as I shall in another place explain ; but the bas-

ket I had never seen before. I felt curious as to his intentions, which turned out to be to dig one row, of a small size, of potatoes which he had bought at a sale or "roup." This surprised me, as I had never before that seen a man in black, with a black neckcloth and no display of linen but a ruffled breast, digging potatoes ; and I felt hurt. I had often experienced the benefit of his style of dressing, for it had many a time kept "blackguard boys" off me —serving as a scarecrow or "potato boggle" for that purpose, even under provocation. The row yielded very few potatoes, not worth carrying home ; and I thought that I might have had them presented to me while in the ground to divide them among the herds, who generally stole their potatoes by digging them with their hands while allowing the vines to stand. This was doubtless a case of bidding at a "roup" at which he had accidentally found himself ; or a whim of a man whose official duties sometimes did not take up all of his time. It had some resemblance to his once "clipping a sheep," when he sent for a sheet and cut my hair in the open air ; and which I shortly afterwards found as the inner lining of a chaffinch's nest. It could not have been for economy, for at all other times I had had my hair cut by an old weaver, in one of the closes of Inverkeithing, whose charge I think was a halfpenny for a child, and a penny for a grown-up person.

We had nothing to complain of at home, for what might be called the discipline of the family was reasonable, and reasonably although strictly carried out. There was nothing of the nature of caprice or arbitrariness, and far less of cruelty, although occasionally punishment might have been less frequently and more leniently administered. Familiarity was certainly not the rule ; but when it was not indulged in, nothing offensive took its place. There was sufficient of it to confirm and intensify the affection on the part of the children which nature implanted in their breasts; and for the rest they were allowed every reasonable privilege of children. Hence the affection on the part of the children was accompanied by that feeling of obedience which was proper to be shown to a father; and in which fear in the offensive sense of the word had no place. There was something that seemed reasonable, or not unreasonable, which we had to do, or take the consequences, which, however, left no hard feelings behind them. He was the superintendent, and it was only occasionally that he had to appear to preserve order. He never interfered with matters in the house that came within the sphere of a woman's duties, for with these he would never trouble himself.

We had at all times a full-grown, sensible and experienced woman in the family that could be relied on, and that could make herself useful in every way as regards housework and the care of children; but we did not keep them long, for they got married, and left with the good-will of us all, and "tea things" costing probably a pound on each occasion. I believe we had three sisters in succession. All these, being so well treated, never forfeited the confidence placed in them; and I do not recollect of an unpleasant circumstance in connection with them. They certainly were a little arbitrary with us boys, as they would scrub us of a Saturday morning in a tub in the little nursery; but there was our father for them to appeal to if we got obstreperous, which on that account seldom happened. They might grab us by the back of the neck and wash us sharply in the tub, or dip us in the sea less gently than they might have done, but we never complained. The complaint was more apt to come from those attending to us.

They were generally decided kind of women, with not the most forbearing of tempers, as on one occasion

I remember, when my brother next youngest to me, between three and four years old, required attendance, which was of frequent occurrence. We were playing on a very warm day, at the edge of the bay where the water was shallow; and I called to Mary, who came like a tigress, and tore the clothes off the child, and, seizing him by the leg and arm, threw him into the water, and waded in after him, and washed him, and carried him on one arm, and his clothes on the other, into the house, which was close to where we were. On another occasion, pretty much all the children were sitting at the east side of the Lazaretto wall, when the child mentioned accidentally got well down the pier, and we were all afraid that he would run over it. But Mary, with great tact, called him by name, with the promise of an apple; and gave him a good spanking on his reaching her. Mary was of the age at which women are said to be desperate; but she got a husband, one much younger than herself.

I recollect in particular one of these "maids," as they were called— Lillie, a fair-haired, blue-eyed, and prepossessing young woman, rather small in size, but of nerve and decision. However sharply she managed me, I never then or at any subsequent time had any feelings of resentment against her than if she had been my mother. She was a woman of tact. On one occasion, when in the kitchen, I objected to go to church, and she said that even the birds had gone to the church; and sure enough there were about twenty sparrows sitting around a blackbird in the leafless hedge—probably from a hawk being near. And when I objected to take my porridge with "molasses" (treacle diluted with water) when milk was scarce, she said that I should not do that, for if I took the molasses I would have a beard as black as Mr. Cobban's when I grew up.* In this

* This Mr. Cobban was in the Customhouse at Inverkeithing, and was trans-

way was the difficulty, got over in both instances.

My mother, with her large family following each other so closely, stood in need of all the assistance which such women could give her. In every way we were well looked after; and there was not an accident worth speaking of that befell any of us except the trifling ones to myself, as I shall relate.

After being ready to start for school, when I was about six years old, I had been playing on a stone the top of which presented a sharp declivity. I slipped off it, and striking on my chin, drove my teeth through my tongue, or cut it badly. Still I was packed off to the school. My tongue certainly felt sore, and particularly when I came to eat my midday bread and butter, in the house of the kindly old family midwife. The occasion was very trying, for there was the appetite which could not be gratified; but she said, " Let me see what a little sugar put on the butter will do," which helped me wonderfully.—On another occasion, when between eight and nine, I was on a tree behind our house, and one of my sisters dared me to jump from it. " Yes," I said, " I'll jump if I should break my neck." There was no real danger that could arise from the height, but the branch from which I leaped being unsteady, led to the accident. My next conscious moment was awaking in bed, with my mother, father and uncle hanging over me. I afterwards learned that I was stunned on reaching the ground, which brought out my mother; but that before she reached me I got on my feet, and ran around the most part of the Lazaretto wall before I was caught. I was out the same day, certainly the next one, as usual.

The other instance can hardly be considered an accident. The inner bay or harbour of Inverkeithing is left

dry at low water, and the muddy surface presents a wretched contrast to the scene when the tide has returned, and is at its height. One day on going home from school, with bag on back, I turned up my trousers as far as they could go, and started across from the bottom of the manse garden in the direction of Pinkie well. When nearly halfway over my imagination became possessed by the idea of bogs and the bottomless pit; and it seemed the same if I tried to turn back or proceed. I kept on my way, and got out at " Pinkie," and there washed my little shanks in the pool at which cows were watered, none the worse, and less disposed to repeat the feat.

After the cholera disappeared the Lazaretto was used for no other purpose than any occasional one the family might have for it. The wooden building, with its three stories, was a fine playing place for the elder children, and the stone building for all the children, in wet weather; and the ground inside the wall served the same purpose when it was dry. Hens when they had chickens were put inside of the wall to protect them against the weasels, which were common outside, in consequence of which we had no rats about the premises; at least I never saw but one, when it was dead and being dragged by a weasel. The family monthly washing was done in a room of the stone building; and twice a year a fire was kindled under a large pot on the ground to furnish water to wash blankets and such things, in the open air, and in the Scotch fashion. I also had the use of the premises for my pigeons and rabbits.

For several years before we left, in 1835, all that was inside of the wall was comprised in the following :—two hand-trucks, a large swivel-musket, a sail soiled by pigeons, a pot and a tin each half-full of tar, in which I found a hen and a blackbird, sitting as on a nest, long dead, but well preserved, and a small pot with

---

ferred to that at Alloa, I believe, about 1833. He had remarkably large and bushy black whiskers.

about an inch of brown paint, nearly as thick as putty, and a brush. The last use I made of the place was to kill, for the table, the rabbits I had running at large. Between the ends of the wooden building and the wall were two high palings (with gates), which divided the ground nearly in two; while a net ran along the back of the building, where there was an open space between the bottom of it and the ground. These made a division suitable for chickens. The paling, being private property, was used to brace our furniture for shipping.

On one occasion my mother used the Lazaretto as a lock-up or prison for myself, but on what provocation I do not remember. One day we noticed the boat of Captain —— leaving Inverkeithing, evidently to pay us a visit. My mother immediately seized me by the collar and proceeded to "put me in quarantine"; but in place of acting more like a pig when laid hold of than a lamb when handled, I went laughing and capering before her, which evidently disconcerted her. I immediately availed myself of the knowledge acquired when investigating the premises to ascertain how our neighbour's cat had reached my rabbits, and got on the wall and dropped from it on the S. W. corner, where it was not so high as at other parts of it. I then received the Captain and Bessie and Bobbie as they landed, and brought them up to the house, precisely as if nothing had happened; not daring to cast a questionable glance at my mother, for fear of making things worse than they had been. However, I was never "put in quarantine" again.

Isolated as we lived, there were few incidents to record in our history. I remember, when the ground was deeply covered with snow, the pier leading to the Lazaretto being used, in the winter of 1831, for salting and barrelling herrings, of which there was a large catch in the firth. The fish were transferred from the boats to a sloop, and there gutted before finding their way into barrels on the pier.—The next summer, or it may have been the summer of that year, I had the opportunity of seeing how kelp was made in all its processes, which were few. There were people who cut, with the ordinary reaping-hook, sea-weed growing on the rocks; a little of which was got inside of the harbour, and the rest on the rocks between the pier and Port Laing sands. This was floated as the tide rose, with a rope thrown around it, and towed to land by a boat. It was then treated exactly as hay is cured, and burned in a round stone circle of moderate height; when the residue, after being puddled by iron rods, became the kelp of commerce.— It was an interesting sight to see the seine hauled. There was one end of the net fastened to the shore, and the boat making a half circle till it landed the other end of it, when both ends were brought together. The fish were then collected, and those not wanted thrown away or into the sea.

I recollect but one instance of a person fishing with the rod. Being a stranger, I watched him closely as he approached the place with his rod and basket. He was an elderly man, dressed in something like port-wine-coloured clothes, with a black dress hat, and spectacles. It was a very blustering day, and he fixed his tackle in Daniel Nicol's byre, and tied the bait, consisting of the inside of crabs, on his hooks with wool; but he did not apparently get a bite. The most he could do was to keep his hat on, and prevent himself from being blown over the pier. I stuck to him from his arrival to his departure, and treated him deferentially, for he looked like a man that might be allowed to go anywhere. With this he seemed pleased; but not a word passed between us.

Between Port Laing sands and where we lived there was a bed of tangle, that was exposed during spring-tides, and in which were many urchins and hermit crabs. It was interesting to see the latter moving about on the sand in the clear and shallow water. I thought I had seen every kind of animal that was to be found there; and I felt surprised on observing an old man, on several occasions, returning past our house from the direction of this tangle-bed, generally with two lobsters, animals that I had never seen before. He was a queer-looking body, in corduroy knee-breeches, brown cloth coat, and dark cloth cap, with a tree leg having a large leathern socket, in which rested his knee, which was amputated a little below the joint. He seemed to be a pensioner, living somewhere in the neighbourhood. He carried a hooked stick of hawthorn, apparently to pull out the lobsters from below or between the rocks. I never could ascertain how or where he got them, and I used to watch for him when the time of low water allowed me to be on the spot. I asked him on the first occasion I saw him where he got the lobsters, but he declined telling me; and I concluded that, to avoid discovery, he went to the place by making a detour by land, to prevent me following him. And yet he would appear with his lobsters. On one occasion I was examining one of them very closely, and before I could profit by his advice it caught me by one of my fingers, which made a lasting impression on my memory.

I never got the length of fishing beyond catching crabs, among the rocks, with a string having bait tied to the end of it.—It was always an interesting occasion to go to Port Laing sands with the man who had charge of the stake-nets there, and see him collect the salmon caught in them.—Sometimes the crew of a boat from a man-of-war would land at the pier, and attract our special attention. I recollect one in particular doing it in grand style when compared with the way of the old quarantine boatmen.—Occasionally a large steamer would arrive at St. Davids for coals, and blow off her steam, which always interested us.— Our maid Lillie had a brother who was a sailor, and who always came ashore to see her on the arrival of the vessel on which he was a hand. We stood in considerable awe of the "sailor," yet when I afterwards thought of his appearance and manner, I came to the conclusion that he was more timid when in our house (with a man in black inside) than we were.—I remember the pinnace from Leith arriving just as it was getting dark, and missing the channel near the entrance of the harbour, and getting aground, well on towards low water, with the wind blowing from the east. The men on board instantly jumped into the water and tried to push the boat into the channel, and failing in that, indulged in a wonderful amount of cursing and swearing.—On one occasion two fishing-boats left Inverkeithing in company, but had not got more than half-way out of the harbour before the crews began to fight from their boats alongside of each other. It was the first fight between men I had ever seen, or rather *heard*, for they were at some distance from me. They were evidently too drunk to do each other much injury with their fists; but they made a horrible noise. The leading spirit, who had children at the school I attended, acted as if he had been crazy; and I still remember the name he applied to one of his opponents.—We were frequently annoyed by careless shooting from the other side of the harbour; two instances of which I recollect. One was a ball passing the right ear of our maid when washing the steps outside of the door, and flattening itself on one of them close at her hand; and the other was one passing through a window of our sitting-room, and striking the wall opposite it.

The island of Inchcolm, between

two and three miles east of St. Davids, appeared from the back of our place as if it made part of the coast line; but as we moved a little towards Port Laing sands a thread of water would appear to separate it from the mainland; a little further would show that a ladder would bridge the two; and the distance would become greater and greater as we kept moving in the same direction. This was always a subject of interest to us.—The appearance of the lands of the Earl of Rosebery, on the opposite side of the firth, from Barnbougle Point to the west, also interested us greatly.

I do not remember having seen a goose in Inverkeithing, and was not aware of the existence of the animal, although the word was frequently enough bandied about among people. Chickens and turkeys and ducks I had seen, as well as the ordinary sea fowls, whether flyers or swimmers, that never or hardly ever entered the harbour. On one very pleasant day, and when the tide was full, I noticed two enormously large white birds fly almost over my head (which at first scared me) and light on the water. With their snow-white plumage, black bills, and large and graceful appearance, they presented a grand sight, floating a little inside of the entrance of the almost land-locked little inlet. This was the first time I saw a swan.

My next grand sight, which did not turn out so pleasantly, was observed a little behind the farm-house, in a small strip of ground in which were a few young trees, and considerable grass. As I had never seen such a phenomenon before, I instantly looked up with astonishment. Here was a young man dressed in a port-wine-coloured coat, white vest and trousers, white beaver hat, polished boots, light-coloured gloves, and brilliant cane, with an amazingly pompous and imposing air. He stood looking at me while I stared at him in wonder, when he bawled out, "What are you doing there, you young scoundrel?" "Seeking nests,

sir," said I in fear. "Come out," said he, "and be ready to go to Dunfermline jail with me to-morrow morning, immediately after breakfast."[*] It was a long time before I recovered from this fright; and morning after morning I was in the utmost dread of the appearance of the man to carry out the punishment threatened. This young man was in all probability the nephew of the absentee owner.

From our house we could recognize people leaving Inverkeithing that we knew, and much more easily when they left the high-road and came along the beach in our direction. My father, being about five feet and nine inches in height, and stout-built, and dressed in black, could easily be made out as he left the town; and his coming always caused a pleasure at home. The view as far as the high-road might have extended over half a mile, and gave us time to prepare for visitors, or consider in the event of the people being strangers. About half-way the road took a slight turn, so that the passenger for a very short time disappeared from view. On going home on one occasion, in wet weather, and long after the school had been dismissed, I made this turn, and remained there with a herd-boy, at the west end of some ruinous houses, situated a little off the path, but to which access could be had through a gap in a dry stone fence, just where we were standing. It seems that my father had seen me coming along the beach and felt impatient at my not emerging from where the road took the turn; and had gone to see what had become of me. However that might be, the herd-boy and I felt for a moment paralyzed on seeing him pop his head through the gap, and turn it upon us without uttering a word. I naturally stood stock-still,

---

[*] This was the identical language used by Daniel Nicol, as I have related. It seems to have been the current phrase of the neighbourhood.

but the herd instantly ran, throwing off his cloak to facilitate his flight, when my father started after him, but soon gave up the chase. We then went home in the best of humour, without any allusion to what had happened; but next morning I had some trouble in allaying the herd-boy's fears. "Why did you run?" said I. "Because I was afraid," he replied. "And why were you afraid?" I continued. To that he could make no reply. My father had only gone to bring me home in the wet weather; the rest was but a whim of what I have already said was at times a half-idle man.

There was a man who visited our house whose nominal calling was that of a slater, but he was useful for a variety of purposes, including that of chimney-sweeping. He would even shoot rooks for those who wanted them for pies, and would find them a hare at almost any time. I was particularly attached to him, for he would bring me wild young rabbits, which I would put inside of the Lazaretto wall among my tame ones. He was a peculiar-looking man, with a wide-awake aspect, but in his way attractive, and well liked—in short, everybody's body; and on animals generally he was a great authority. He might have been forty years old, and was remarkably active; and in the summer season he was generally clothed in something like coarse linen. When he visited us on business, of some kind or other, it was always early in the morning, and by crossing the bay when the tide was out. He was invariably accompanied by a handsome bull-terrier, which was apparently so trained that it would not, under almost any provocation, even touch a cat unless set on it by its master. It was always a subject of interest to us children when the dog arrived. It never caused any disturbance in the kitchen, beyond the sullen and zizzag retreat of the cat—yet never showing a full brush— as the dog devoured the contents of its dish—apparently its breakfast—to which it was always made welcome.

I coveted this dog, which I found one morning, on my way to school, hunting by itself, and "within the limits." I coaxed it to return with me, and had it locked up till I returned in the afternoon, but with no definite idea of anything beyond that. On the N. E. corner of the Lazaretto wall, facing the East Ness, was a double-leafed door leading into a small passage; on the right side of which was the boatmen's house, and on the left the superintendent's office, both disused. There was a scuttle on the roof of this passage, leading to a small loft, which, to my sorrow, I never had the opportunity of rummaging, to see whether it contained spy-glasses or such things. In the space between the two rooms I confined the dog. I took little interest in what passed at school that day, for my thoughts were given to the dog, and the pleasure I would have on getting home; without a thought of what was due to the dog, or as if it had any rights. I was unconscious of having done a wrong to any one, or of having any unsettled troubles on hand; and I fiercely demanded of my mother, "What have I been doing now?" as she, without saying a word, began to give me what, in the language of the place, was called a "tabbering," immediately on my entering the house. "I'll teach you to put a nasty dog into my milk-house," was her reply. I denied the charge, and stuck to my denial. I really was not aware of the boatmen's watch-house having been used for any purpose, as it must have been visited only during school hours; the real milk-house being attached to our dwelling-house. I said that "I did *not* put a nasty dog into your milk-house." She had no proof but "habit and repute, and the nature of things," and insisted on a confession; which I at last made by saying, "No, I did not put a nasty dog into your *milk-house;* I only put it into the *lobby.*" I never learned how the dog was released. It might have been by its howling, or on my mother going to the milk-house, when it would bolt out, leaving no doubt in her mind how it had got there.

I had to be more cautious with my father in regard to a bull-dog to which I took a fancy. In a place like Inverkeithing, all kinds of children attending the parish school mixed with each other; it was only in the houses, or under special circumstances, that class appeared. I had little choice of companions, and had to take whatever came my way. My father said to me that he had no objection to me "strolling the country with blackguard boys of my own age, or even with big blackguard boys; but for me to stroll with a big blackguard boy *and a bull-dog* was what he would not permit." I thought his objection to the bull-dog was unreasonable, and I disregarded his orders. It was a large white and yellow dog, covered, like a blackguard, with the remains of wounds received in many a battle; which added to my regard and respect for it. It seemed as if I were getting a share in the dog, without the trouble and expense of keeping it. I thought that Will, whom it followed, and I and the dog were fit for anything. We had a stroll one Saturday afternoon, and, when tired, laid down on the grass, near the road leading to the Ferry, face downwards, and resting our foreheads on our arms, but without going to sleep. One of my sisters, unknown to me, saw us when passing, and reported the case to my father. I walked with Will on his way home for nearly half a mile beyond the spot where I should have left him; and lingered there while arranging for our stroll on the following Saturday, in another direction. On arriving at home I avoided my father's presence, but was sent for, and to my dismay charged with having been found "sleeping with the big blackguard boy and his bull-dog

on the Ferry Hills." The charge was too true and too unexpected, and the danger too great, for me to raise a question as to our having been *sleeping;* and so I said nothing. I got off on the promise of dropping the dog's acquaintance for the future. I still kept up that with Will, against whom personally no objection was taken; but I did not venture to ask whether I might stroll with him and a dog that was not a bull-dog.

I have already said that my father was reasonable in such matters, although I did not *then* think that his objection to the bull-dog was so. I might even characterize his government as that of an amiable, sensible, and constitutional despotism, from which there was no appeal. And this is what should be shown by every one having the responsibility of bringing up children, especially when they are of a certain age.

I recollect, when I was about seven years old, being at home sick — possibly of scarlet fever—in which case I remember I was only one day in bed, so light was the attack. I was playing with a wooden hammer at the window on the stair leading to the top floor, where there were some pots of flowers, and I accidentally broke a pane of glass. Under ordinary circumstances this was a capital offense, in consequence of the price of glass, when there was a heavy duty on it. I prudently went to bed shortly before my father's coming home; and when he approached the room in which I was I began to snore, while listening attentively to what might be said. In his allusion to my sickness my father said, "Poor fellow!" which was satisfactory enough; but the trying part about the broken pane had yet to come. However, my mother brought it up under extenuating circumstances, which decided the question; but I still kept snoring till my father shook me up to know how I felt.

My father's repeated injunction to us was, that when we did anything wrong we were to tell him ; which we were always ready enough to do when we had to meet the consequences from any one outside. I remember one occasion in particular. The boy who occasionally herded the sheep near our house, to which I have alluded, left me late on a Saturday night, with a bright fire and a roast of potatoes under it, which I ate, and dispensed with supper in consequence. He certainly had treated me with great kindness, yet for some unaccountable reason I destroyed everything, after having eaten the potatoes, that were all but ready when he left me. I had no sooner got to our house, which was at a very short distance, than I regretted what I had done, not merely on account of its baseness, but for the dread of the consequences ; and before going to bed I told my father everything. He then gave me a penny, which I was to take to the boy the first thing I did on Monday morning ; and say that it was from him, and that I was sorry for what I had done. The boy—a big fellow, with a cast in one of his eyes—received the penny with pleasure ; and we continued friends as if nothing had happened. Still, I would drive his sheep at night, and ride the biggest of them that I could lay hold of.

In regard to our intercourse with other boys, my father's peremptory orders went no further than that we were not to annoy them, or be aggressors in any way. The rest, although never in any way expressed or implied, was left to ourselves ; so that if we gave "two for one" to those that annoyed us or proved aggressors, or hunted them out of the neighbourhood, we never had a thought of trouble at home on that account.

As may be easily imagined, we were all intensely loyal. The King was a being of whom I could form no conception beyond his being something like the father of everybody, and the maker of all the money. With this undefined and exalted idea of a king, it was with awe that I went to visit what passed in the neighbourhood for the "king o' the leears," to see whether I could do him obeisance ; but what a shock it gave to my feelings of reverence, and what a contempt it raised against such as admitted *him* to be their king !

The subject of ghosts I never heard alluded to in our house. It must have been purposely kept from us. Even Halloween I never heard mentioned ; and the only idea we had of Hogmanay was some extra fancy bread on the evening of the last day of the year. As a natural consequence, when I went to school I had never heard of ghosts, and was therefore sceptical of them. I remember one boy with whom I had many a discussion on the subject. "Where are they to be found ?" I said. "Well," said he, "there is one, in the house at the East Ness," a building then vacant, and which afterwards became the Custom-house. This was coming rather near us, for the house was opposite ours, on the other side of the narrow entrance to the harbour, and had been (to a child) long uninhabited ; which had given rise to a rather uncanny feeling, for even to a grown-up person the ideas associated with such a building are not pleasant. I pressed the boy with such questions as, "How did he get into the house ? where did he sleep ? and what did he have for bed-clothes ?" And on asking him, "How could I see him ?" he said that there were two ways for calling up the "father of ghosts"—to go to sleep with the bare right arm left outside of the bed-clothes, and by throwing out of a byre three "empty grapefuls" immediately after dark. I tried both, without success—using the fork, already mentioned, with which my father dug a small row of potatoes in a field.

And so far as I recollect, these were the only occasions on which the fork was used after we gave up keeping a cow, which is almost as far back as my memory can carry me.

Although we in a general way despised ghosts, we were always afraid of more tangible beings. Thus I got up one day early in the morning to pull the gooseberries and currants (there was no other fruit) of Daniel Nicol before he and his wife were afoot; but I got up too early, for it was before complete daylight, and I boggled at something that looked like a person sitting with his back against the corner of his house, waiting for me; and I returned to my bed; but when I rose at the usual time I went to see what had frightened me, and found that it was a stone placed there to keep carts off the house, and which I had often seen before. And so, as I have already said, I visited the garden in broad daylight, well on in the forenoon.

What gave us the greatest concern in the way spoken of was the celebrated Dr. Knox, of Burke and Hare notoriety, taking up his quarters with his family, in the autumn of 1835, in the old Cruicks' farm-house. When we passed in that direction during the day we kept as far away from the house as possible; and would not pass close to it unless we were accompanied by a grown-up person. At night the presence of an old person would not completely do away with the fear which we entertained for him as we passed his door. His presence was regarded with great favour by the farmers, whose crops were well protected in consequence from depredators; and they regretted that he did not return the following year. Possibly some of them might have subscribed to pay for his lodgings, which could not have cost much for the old house occupied by him.

Isolated as we lived, gossip was what we relished. We all contributed our shares to the common stock as we came home; and I have no doubt that I furnished a full share. We knew better than trouble our father with such matters, and seldom our mother. Those interested were ourselves and the maid. We were all very industrious in bringing gossip into the house, and as careful that nothing should leave it. But we found that there was a large leak somewhere, which turned out to be the boy next youngest to me; who would stop people and tell everything that took place in the house, and answer questions put to him, in which respect he was a pump that was always "on the fang." This habit annoyed us, and our only remedy was to say nothing in his hearing that we did not wish made public. I felt particularly aggravated when twitted by people with such remarks as that I was "an industrious laddie to get up at three o'clock in the morning to catch mice for the cat's breakfast"; and that I was "a foolish laddie not to let the cat do that for herself." This habit became so notorious in a small place like Inverkeithing, that as we would pass through it on our way to and from school, the women would come out and look at the boy when accompanied by me. On one occasion a number of young women and half-grown girls accosted us, clapping their hands, when one of them, more demonstrative than the others, almost spat out the following: —"If you were brither o' mine I would tie a wisp o' strae about ye, and stap ye up the lum!"—alluding to the habit of putting a bag filled with something in fire-places during the summer, when no fires are used.

The allusion to the cat and the mice for her breakfast came about in this way:—On getting home from school I found puss prostrate, as if her back had been broken, and not able even to crawl. The explanation was that she had arrived from the direction of the farm house, "with the speed of lightning," and never rose after entering the house. On enquiry I found that the thrashing-mill had been started while two cats were mousing there ; which resulted in a terrific yell on the part of one cat, while the farm one was not hurt. In the condition described our cat was an invalid that got the most careful nursing for about fourteen days before she recovered. She was reared, if not born, in the house, and had a name, and was, as it were, one of the family, that never quarrelled with another member of it ; and she had no dog to divide the affection with which we all regarded her, for a dog was not allowed on the premises. Always on coming home from school the first question was, " How is puss, and when will she be on her feet and at her work ? " She ultimately " got on her feet and at her work," which accumulated wonderfully during the interval. If I had had sufficient reflection I would doubtless have caught mice for her " breakfast," or any other of her meals; but it was not necessary to have got up at three o'clock in the morning for that purpose. I had indeed got up early one day in connection with the mice ; which formed the foundation of the taunts referred to. I naturally felt hurt at that, and at the scandal of everything done at home being made the town's talk ; but I had not the redress which a thrashing would give. It was our father's exclusive prerogative in such cases to " do all the thrashing that was wanted " ; but sometimes it was difficult to make out a charge in the way of a complaint. however offensive or provocative the circumstances might be. Hence I would sometimes take pleasure in seeing my brother well thrashed by other boys, when he had thoroughly earned the punishment. At other times I would frighten him, which was sometimes better than beating him, and of which the following is a very fair illustration :—

When in the middle of a young plantation, of about an acre, back of Port Laing sands, and on the line of the small loch to the west of it, I,

unobserved by my brother, withdrew to the outside of it, and raised the cry of " a weasel." I then started for home, and had got near the road that leads to the farm, when two gentlemen stopped me, and asked me impatiently what was the meaning of my running, and of the boy on the brow of the hill running and roaring so loudly as he did. The result was our going home together, and a good behaviour on the boy's part for some time.

From the part of the Ferry Hills alluded to, and looking towards the west, on the same side of the firth, the ruins of Rosyth Castle present a striking object for contemplation. A little before the time I have spoken of, the view was rendered much more sombre by the appearance, towards the left and a little further up St. Margaret's Hope, of five or six quarantine hulks, that is, large men-of-war having nothing but their lower masts and bow-sprits standing. I had often passed Rosyth Castle, but a little inland of it, while going to and from Limekilns, in the company of grown-up people. Scotch boys then were not partial to visiting places that were strange to them, unless when with others that were familiar with them. And I presume the same peculiarity still exists among them. They became suspicious of everybody and everything when strolling out of what might be called their districts. On one occasion I went with two boys to Rosyth hamlet, with the object of visiting one of the hulks referred to, in the event of her boat coming ashore, and in which we expected to be taken to the vessel. We went along the beach, passing sloe-bushes that never bore sloes in my recollection, till we reached the east side of a small creek ; near the head of which was a small foundery, with a few men working in it. Almost immediately opposite was the ruined castle. We waited patiently for the coming of the boat, which did not make its appearance ; and being disappointed at that, we were anxious to pass the foundery, and visit the ruin. But do what we could, we could not muster up courage to pass the foundery; and so we returned as we came. And yet there was no possible chance of any one interfering with us in carrying out our wishes, which were those of children under ten years of age.*

Being disappointed in not being able to visit the ruined castle, owing to our timidity in regard to passing the foundery—the lion in the path—I made up another expedition with two boys. Profiting by experience, we went by the public road, ard reached the ruin west of the dreaded foundery. We got on the first floor, which was easily reached, but we did not try to ascend higher. It was the first ruin of the kind that I had visited; and what struck me was that the floors were of stone; the one up to which we had got being covered by a deep bed of earth and sod. We then started for the Lazaretto. The tide being remarkably high, we had to make a detour to the right, to reach the old houses where my father had appeared so suddenly, and given a herd-boy and myself so terrible a fright. At ordinary times we would have walked on the gravel-beach, and made use of stepping-stones over a "bad bit." Reaching the old houses, we had to make another detour to get round the bight already spoken of. This little bight was the trying part in going to and from our house. Around the west side of it the quarantine boatmen had built an elevated road of about four feet in breadth, consisting of earth with a ragged stone facing, to meet the case of high tides; but it was seldom used, owing to the spongy condition in which it generally was. When the tide was not at its height, stepping-stones were used in its place; not in a straight line from the old houses to our dwelling, but almost parallel with the raised path. After lingering about the little bay (for to a child even a distance of three feet in any direction has a meaning), and contemplating the very high tide which had filled it so completely, we started for the Lazaretto. Nothing particularly attracted the other boy's notice there except that parts of the pier were covered by the scales of herrings that had lain there since the winter of 1831, nearly four years before. And from this it appeared that, in using the pier for cholera purposes, in the summer of 1832, the workmen had cleared away only such part of the refuse of the fish as was necessary for their purpose, and left the remainder to be disposed of by the elements. To be sure, the pier was a public one, and not under the exclusive jurisdiction of the Crown; but I often thought that the boatmen, with so much idle time at their disposal, might have made things look decent, especially as the pier was a small one. But they apparently acted the part which seems to be characteristic of many Government establishments—to touch nothing that does not specially concern the service, and do no more

---

* The feeling alluded to runs through almost every aspect and relation of Scotch life and character. I have never spoken to Scotch people of intelligence and, candour, in America, that did not admit what I have said. They have at heart a feeling of having been cowed from their infancy upwards, in almost every relation of life, that makes them sensitive and reserved, suspicious and timid, however brave and determined they may be when they once "sail in." The feeling in question does not appear to them so plain while they live in Scotland as it does after they leave it, and mix in a community of other people. They have not that confidence and assurance in their movements which would spring from its opposite—impudence and a lack of shame. In that respect I once said to a Scotch lady while on a visit to America:—"You Scotch are blate bodies, that at first appear like sheep that have neither horns in their heads nor tongues in their mouths." "Aye," said she in reply, "but we soon show people that we have both horns in our heads and tongues in our mouths."

even in regard to that than is absolutely necessary.

The occasion of my other expedition to the neighbourhood of Rosyth is not very distinctly impressed on my memory. I recollect coming *from* it, with three boys, walking four abreast—I on the right, a big boy next me, then a boy smaller than myself, and on the outside of the line, a boy nearly of my own size, and with whom I was on the best of terms. Taking advantage of the big boy's friendship for him, he began, without the slightest provocation, to lash me over the back of a bird, the name of which happened to be my nickname. He would step out of the line, in advance (but always keeping the big boy between us), and indulge in the most offensive gestures and language in regard to the bird. The other boys laughed and jeered, and enjoyed themselves amazingly; and left me no alternative but to book everything for a future settlement. For it must be remembered that almost *every person* living in Inverkeithing had a nickname, and was frequently spoken of in public by no other. At the school every boy had such a name, and sometimes more than one; and he was generally called by it, except that small boys would not venture to address big boys by these extra "given names" if they were more than ordinarily offensive. Sometimes the very mention of the nickname would immediately lead to a fight. As illustrative of what I have said, I remember having been considerably frightened by some boys impatiently demanding who had done so and so, that he might be beaten for it, and one calling out the name of the bird I have alluded to; but the others, still impatiently, asked which —— it was. And the reply being ⸻ ——, I felt relieved, for I was the other boy that had been christened after the bird; the name of which was thus the nickname of two boys at least.

I was in no hurry for a settlement, like a person whose claim for principal and accruing interest is well secured; and I never troubled the debtor (who seems to have avoided me) till I met him accidentally between the church and the school, on the opposite side of the street. The narrowness of the space and the configuration of the buildings may have produced the effect, or it may have been an illusion on my part, still I could never divest myself of the idea that the blows on the culprit's ribs sounded like an echo somewhere. This much is certain, that a big boy called "Biscuits" (from his large cheeks of the colour of sailors' biscuits) called out from the opposite side of the street, that if I fought as well as I thrashed, I would do wonders. Still standing with his back at the wall, and roaring for mercy while undergoing "the public administration of law and justice," I said I would let him off if he would tell me of a nest. At this time it was early-spring, which led to the most diligent search for a bird's nest, as something to be boasted of at the school by the fortunate finder of the first one. And that reminds me that the debt spoken of had been contracted about six months before; so that a long forbearance had been shown in the collection of what was generally "cash over the counter." The boy was a great "nester," and he immediately told me where I would find a nest; describing everything so exactly that I had no doubt of his sincerity.

The place where he said the nest was to be found was a little knoll in the middle of a ploughed field. It was a spot to which I took a fancy merely on account of its appearance; and I could never pass it without a pleasant feeling in regard to it for that reason alone. The year before, when passing the upper end of it, on my way home from the farm, when it was all but dark, my eye caught the sight of a whin having one stem, and a round bunch at the top;

which led me to scrutinize it closely, when I found a nest of gray linnets, so full-grown that every one flew out of the nest, on my touching it, but one, which I caught. Daylight was too far gone to allow me to search for the others where they had flown to. I felt satisfied with the one I had secured, in the belief that it was the baby of the family, the last hatched, which was always considered a singer. Next morning I took it down to the sea-shore, where I thought I could try its powers of flight with safety, but I lost it by its getting into a hole in the west side of the pier; which reminds me that the pier was not built at a great expense, for it was composed of stones not very closely laid together, without mortar, on the under part at least. On the lower end of the knoll was the whin bush in which I was told I would find the nest, which the boy gave me as a settlement of the balance of my claim. He described the knoll very accurately, and the bush most minutely, even that it "hung over" the knoll. I had thoroughly searched it a few days before without finding a nest; but one might have been commenced after that. On again searching the bush I found that I had been imposed on.

I cannot say that I felt displeased at the impromptu, circumstantial and successful trick by which the boy deceived me, while he had his back at the wall, and was in the hands of the Philistine. Still, I never spoke of it to him, for fear it might have opened the old sore, which I wished closed, as I really liked the boy, and had often strolled with him; and it was to me a matter of surprise and grief that he should have so "wantonly and wickedly" provoked me in the way he did. We soon became friends as before, and strolled as we had done. His having a hound recommended him greatly to me; for it could not be said that his *size* and the *kind* of his dog came under the description of "boy and dog" forbidden to me by my father.

Shortly after this, I was with this boy and another boy, and the hound, within a few feet of the spot where I had been so greatly frightened by the first "swell" I met with, dressed as he was in a white hat, port-wine-coloured coat, etc., but on the opposite side of the fence, and on another property. The unwritten law between farmers and their herds was that the herd could "pull" anything in a field he took a fancy to, and treat his friend, provided it was eaten on the spot. On this occasion, having no herd with us, we had each pulled a small turnip, at an early stage of its growth, when field turnips are palatable. The value of the three if they had arrived at maturity might not have exceeded a halfpenny, or a penny at the most; but to take such a liberty was against the most peremptory orders at home. I was doubtless led to join in the action by the example of the two boys with me. I was thoroughly conscious of having done wrong, and with that on my mind, and the vivid recollection of having been threatened with being sent to jail by the "swell" referred to, while almost on the same spot, nesting, I was in a condition to be influenced by a panic, which came from a quarter the most unexpected. While we were busily eating the turnips, on our feet and with our backs against a stone dyke, the hound, close by us, but out of sight, set up a howl that I had never heard before; at the sudden and horrible sound of which I instantly dropped the turnip at my feet, speechless. I saw the dog running in our direction and howling, apparently in pursuit of nothing; but on the sharp turn of a furze-lined path, close to me, an animal which it was chasing passed me so closely that I could have kicked it had I had a good conscience and self-possession to realize what it was; for the suddenness of the whole thing did not admit of an instant's reflection. The chase had proceeded some distance past us before I became aware that the dog had started a hare ; when my attention became rivetted to a black and white animal following what had the appearance of a gray thread, as it pursued the hare up a hill, when both disappeared over the top of it. This ended what was to me a real panic. Still I picked up and finished the turnip, which had dropped out of my hands, as if nothing had happened.

This leads me to speak of a hare in the burial of which was the only occasion on which I recollect having seen my father with a spade in his hands, as I have already mentioned. It had become the "rage" among the boys at the school to have cross-bows, with hares' ribs for the bows. I had noticed the boy who had so grossly insulted me, in reference to my having my sister's old shoes on my feet, drop his bow in the school, when I picked it up, and put it under my jacket, as some satisfaction for the offense he had been guilty of. Some time after, he missed his bow, and made a great noise in regard to it ; when I quietly drew it from under my jacket, and innocently said to him, " Is this your gun ? " " Yes," said he, " and where did you get it ? " " On the floor," said I, and gave it to him. If hares had been in season I would have had no difficulty in getting the ribs of them for the purpose mentioned ; but as they were not in season, I endeavoured (industriously and foolishly, as the Inverkeithing wives would have said,) to find a dead hare, by hunting all over the Cruicks' peninsula for one. I spent probably three or four hours on two successive long summer evenings searching every likely and unlikely place in which a dead hare might possibly be found, but without success. A few days afterwards, as I had reached about fifty yards from our gate, on my way to school, my eyes became rivetted on a hare asleep ; and I instantly stopped and contemplated the object for a minute or two. I softly advanced, and yet the hare moved not ; and still nearer, with the same effect. The result was that I got up to the hare and found her in her form dead and cold, precisely as when she had gone to rest. Now, said I, I will have hares' ribs enough for a cross-bow; and returned with the animal, and put it inside of a sow's house, then in disuse. On coming home from school my father demanded of me what I had done with the dead hare, when I produced it ; and I told him, in answer to his question, what use I intended to make of it. He then entered the Lazaretto and buried the hare in my presence, saying, as he tramped the earth on it, " Now, sir, that hare lies there." " Yes, sir," said I in reply. I felt greatly disappointed ; but what my father did was right. I had the most crude ideas about getting the ribs of a dead hare ; for as I had seen the carcass of a horse behind the Lazaretto rot, after it had been shot and skinned, so I thought I could get the ribs of the hare after it had become corrupted, and the ribs could be separated from the rest of the body. I have often thought since of the coincidence of finding the dead hare under the circumstances mentioned ; saying nothing of what is doubtless a rarity in natural history —that of getting a hare dead in precisely the same position in which it had gone to rest in its form.

My finding a halfpenny in a hen-house was under more questionable circumstances. I crossed to the East Ness, when the tide was out, on my way to school ; and as I passed the bridge that leads to the harbour wynd I climbed up a narrow ladder that admitted chickens into their roost, which adjoined a large old-fashioned white house, on the right, and closer to the water. I had no apparent motive for what I did ; it certainly was not to take eggs, which I would have scorned to do. However, I put in my hand at the hole through which the chickens entered from the street, while the door of the roost was behind ; and I carefully scraped, with my hand, the landing place from which the fowls apparently hopped to their perches. To my astonishment I drew out a halfpenny, which I spent on a stick of "black man." I carefully scraped the same place, unsuccessfully, three or four days in succession, to find another halfpenny ; which I would not have done had I known more of the "doctrine of averages" relating to "finding a halfpenny in a hen-house" every day of the week, unless it might have happened that another boy had used the place as a bank in which he kept his money. This happened a little before nine o'clock in the morning, and alongside of the dwelling-house ; and it was the only hen-roost that I troubled in any way.

As another illustration of what a child will sometimes do without any apparent motive, I may mention that I removed from the Lazaretto "a small pot, with about an inch of brown paint, nearly as thick as putty, and a brush," already mentioned; and put it back in the same place the following day. I had no intention of making any use of the paint-pot. The key of the quarantine premises was always at the disposal of any one of the family, and was daily used by me in connection with my pigeons and rabbits ; so that if I wanted the paint-pot I could have got it at any time. I put it back for safety, and never thought anything further about it.

The greatest fright I ever experienced was connected with my second school-bag. With the first I innocently had had trouble enough. This bag (made of leather) was the only one that had appeared at the school, and therefore had attracted special notice. One of the big boys, unknown to me, printed my name and address, in the largest-sized letters, on the outside of the bag, taking the idea from the knapsacks of some soldiers that had been billeted in the town while on their march. And it appears that I had gone home all the way from school with the bag on my back, and the name outside. My father felt greatly provoked, and had the writing taken off by the shoemaker who made the bag, and had my name written inside. In this condition I used it for a short time, and then I got another bag ; in connection with which I got the fright alluded to.

The school was dismissed at four o'clock, and I could easily get home, even allowing for a little gossip, by half-past four. One day I did not reach home till about half-past eight, with no thought on my mind but what I should get to eat on my arrival. But before I had even put a foot on the outer step, the door, to my astonishment, was abruptly opened by my father (who seems to have scrutinized me while coming up the walk) with the demand of "Your bag, sir? where's your bag?" I instinctively applied my hands to my flanks, and said, "My bag? Aye, where's my bag?" "Don't let me see you come into my house without your bag," was my father's reply. I had nothing to do for it but to return on my tracks, and find the unfortunate satchel. I carefully thought of every place I had stopped at, and scrutinized it unsuccessfully, till I reached a well on the beach, near the foundery, where I had lingered a good while with another boy, and where I felt all but certain that I had the bag. I made a diligent search for it in every direction, without success; and my heart sank within me as I thought of what I had heard : "Your bag, sir? where's your bag?" I had visited so many places before arriving at the well, in the first instance, during the previous four hours, that I could not think in what particular direction I should go in a further search ; and it never occurred to me that my name being on a well-known bag would lead to its return by the finder. I sat down on the well, the picture of misery, when I thought of what I had been told: "Don't let me see you come into my house without your bag." But I did not weep, for I kept my tears for the "wallcp'ng" which I would get on going home without the bag. As a temporary relief to my feelings, I began to think of the well, and how I had seen it built, visiting it almost a'ways twice a day, on my way to and from school, as if I had been the inspector to see that the job had not been scamped. It was indeed a substantial piece of work, of large, well-hewn hard white sandstone, and well puddled with clay, and oblong in shape, running in the direction of the shore line.

I h₁ve said that I felt all but certain that I had my bag when at the well; but whether that was so or not, I passed round the harbour to the third or fourth house on the crescent to see the boy, with whom, a short time before, I had lingered at the well. He was three or four years older than myself, and had rich dark russet hair, a wonderfully freckled complexion, and black eyes of the greatest brilliancy. He was a very popular boy, and I never knew of his having trouble with any one. I presume that, like other people there, especially boys, he had a nickname; but I never heard it, unless it was the one he generally went by, that is, his surname curtailed.

I told him everything, and what I had done; and he satisfied me that I had the bag on my back at the well when I left him, which did not help me. I begged him to return with me to the well, which he readily did with the greatest kindness and sympathy, although he said that he did not see what use he could be to me there. "But only come," said I, with no idea of any assistance he could be to me. We then returned to the well, and searched unsuccessfully in every direction. By this time it was nearly dark, with not a creature moving;

still, we lingered at the well in absolute silence; I averse to start for home without the bag, and he as unwilling to leave me in my forlorn and wretched state. The silence was broken, and our attention arrested, by a boy of my own size approaching from the direction of the manse garden, with a long step and at a rapid pace. "Hollo, what have you got there?" said my friend to the boy as he observed something like a string hanging a little down from under his buttoned jacket, just as he was passing us. The result was that the boy approached, and unbuttoned his jacket, showing my bag, which he had found at the back of the hedge between the well and the manse garden, about seventy yards from where we stood. "Yes," said I, "I put it down there before climbing up to a blackbird's nest, in which I found nothing." The appearance of the bag was the end of all trouble, for I knew that there would be no reproaches when I got home. My only and immediate thought was about what I would find to fill my little crop at that time of night. I did not enter the house with the vapouring air of, "My bag sir? why, there's my bag!" but I dutifully produced it, with an account of where and how I had found it; when I received advice to be more careful, and to come home earlier, for the future. I then proceeded to my dinner and supper rolled into one, and went to bed absolutely happy.

I felt extremely grateful to the boy mentioned. The last time I remember seeing him was when he came across to our place, on a Saturday afternoon, in the summer of 1835, when the tide was out. We then sat talking about various matters by the hedge at the bottom of our garden (so-called), when my eldest sister was practising her piano lessons, on the upper floor, with the windows up.

I have mentioned all the troubles which I can remember having had at home. There were doubtless others, of a minor importance, or presenting no salient points by which they could be recollected. In going to and from church my place was to walk alongside of my mother, which, however, did not prevent me from noticing anything that I could examine on the following day. For a good part of the distance (about half a mile) between our house and the high-road, we had to walk Indian file, along the narrow paths, or on the stepping-stones on parts of the beach, when I would have to take the advance. On one occasion, when going up a narrow and crooked path from the valley (which an athlete could almost have leaped over) to the high ground (which rose about twelve feet), I had almost a fight with my mother. I was in advance, and had noticed a foggie-bee about to alight, the meaning of which I well understood. I instantly stopped and, making way for the others to pass, turned round to see the exact spot where the bee would disappear, when the trouble began. I was seized by the arm, and after some resistance dragged along, while looking behind; but I managed to see the bee get under the leaf of a thistle. I dwelt on the circumstance while at church, and carefully noticed the leaf of the thistle, without daring to touch it, on my return home. On Monday morning I discovered the nest which I felt sure was there.—When very young I brought into the house the nest of a wren in which was a large progeny, when my mother, with an expression of pain which I could never forget, told me to place it where I had found it; which I did.

Opposite the entrance to the Lazaretto was a well, the roof of which consisted of stone slabs, sloping to the ground in the direction of the town; while its upright entrance faced east. It was so near the sea that the water would become unfit for use by occasional very high tides, when the well would have to be emptied. This was apparently the grounds of an action raised by the town against the person who bought the property from the Government, alleging that the well was within high-water mark. The real reason seems to have been enmity between the parties. One of the old boatmen told me afterwards that he had been cited as a witness in the action, on the part of the proprietor, when I asked him what *he* knew about the well; and he said that he ought to know something about it, for that he had "bigged" it. He said that he had tried to find the spring inside of the Lazaretto wall, but failed. I always understood that the town was beaten in the action, which it well deserved to be, for the well was built by the Crown, and was the only one on or near the premises; and did not, in any reasonable sense of the word, come under the phrase, "within high-water mark." It was always kept locked, apparently to prevent the children from falling into it; and also for the reason that, isolated as we lived, people would sometimes take liberties with it. Thus I remember a sailor washing his feet in it, which caused no small indignation to all about the place. This was the well out of which my father drew the water to throw over Daniel Nicol's cow, as Lizzie or Pussie Nicol raced it backwards and forwards, to cure it of the effects of it having eaten too freely of wet clover, as I have already mentioned. Some of my earliest and most pleasant recollections are connected with this well.

The next well, to the west, was at the bottom of a hollow (called "the valley"), and near the sea; the one in which Giles regarded frogs with such aversion, as I have stated. But this well had always a wretched appearance. A few yards west of that was "Pinkie," to which I have already made allusion. The boatman mentioned said that he was also at the building of "Pinkie," and that he tried to find the spring further up the hill. This well was very small, but prettily built; and was so surrounded by whins that it was hardly observable until search was made for the source of the pool out of which stock were watered. This pool was merely a hollow dug out, while nature did the rest, giving it a fringe and surroundings, as if the hand of man had not been there. A little further west, and at the bottom of the land of the Cruicks' farm, was a well, all but covered by a flat roof on a level with the ground, that supplied the old farm-house and formerly a small row of houses near the beach (already referred to), which were in ruins in my time, but which had consisted of three distinct apartments, with as many entrances.

Pinkie well is connected in my memory with many associations. The well, as I have said, was in itself attractive. Its water was used in the baptism of all our family; the font being a milk-bowl of little more than ordinary ware, but of a handsome form, and prettily decorated in blue, with a woman milking a cow at the bottom, of superior design and execution. Whenever our own well was injured by the sea entering it, we always had recourse to "Pinkie"; but it was too far off for ordinary purposes, superior as the water was. When going to school I would fill a pitcher at "Pinkie" for the use of my father at the Custom-house. There was another interest connected with this well, that it was the only running spring on the peninsula that I knew of. If there was another, it must have been between St. Margaret's Point on the west and the Ferry on the east; but I do not think that there was a running spring there.

There was a good show of trees inside of the Lazaretto wall, as well as on the ground adjoining, where there was also a profuse growth of ivy. These attracted the birds, for they had no other foliage on the peninsula to resort to, except three or four wretched old pines at the Ferry; a recent plantation on the brow of the village; about an acre of young wood above Port Laing sands, already referred to; about a dozen of scraggy trees and bushes scattered over the rest of the district; and a few small hawthorns in two small hedges.

I do not remember when I first went to school, or any of the circumstances connected with it. I presume it must have been in the spring or summer of 1831, for when the school was dismissed in 1832, in consequence of the cholera, I was conscious of having been for some time at it. I also remember that previously, when the vacation had come round, I was packed off to a school kept by two sisters—one much younger than the other, and called "wasp-waisted ———," in consequence of tight lacing. This school was opposite to the church and parish school, but nearest the church, and up a flight of stone steps, in the open air, that led to an old-fashioned house on the left; while there was a modern one on the right. The school-room was three or four steps up into the old house, to the left, with the window to the street, above the spot where I caught the culprit mentioned. I thought it hard to be sent to this school after the children of the other one had been dismissed to play; and I was either removed or I left because the vacation for this one had also come round. I am sure that my industry for learning was not the cause of my being kept so closely at school; it might have been to get rid of me at home; but of doing anything deserving of that, I was never conscious.

I might have seen the play-ground of the school before going to it; but the great probability is that I did not, or did not remember it. When I first saw the play-ground, that part of it on the upper end, of a triangular form, was neatly laid out in shrubs, all around the wall and railing, with a triangular walk separating these shrubs from some in the centre of the ground.

In front of the end window was a semi-circular clump of shrubs. There were also trees (all of one kind) around the sides of this part of the ground, and in front of the school, and at least one (I think two) behind it. But very soon everything disappeared but the trees, of which the teacher took great care.

The teacher was about thirty-one years old when I went to the school, and thirty-five when I left it. He was a licentiate of the church, teaching a school till he could find a charge, which he did a few years after the establishment of the Free Church. When I was at his school I remember hearing him preach at Dalgety, the adjoining parish, to the east. He was always styled "The Reverend," and he was very particular to let it be understood that he was a "Preacher of the Word." He was unmarried, and had his sister as housekeeper. In his person he was short and a little pursy, but gentlemanly, and had dark (but not black) hair and eyes. There were four gay people in Inverkeithing at this time: the teacher; a rather uppish and extravagant but popular farmer of middle age (from the same place in Fife as the teacher) ; a tall, fine-looking, fair and florid, and gallant young doctor, who married a widow with four well grown-up children, and a good annuity, which "went out at the door as the doctor came in " ; and the fashionable and handsome young wife of a manufacturer, who was advanced in years, and had to be drawn about in a hand-coach. Among these four there was nothing but gayety—eating and drinking and singing, music and dancing and card-playing, with *guising* in its season.

The teacher had not reached the goal of his aspiration—a church, and in the meantime had become a dominie all over. At his own table he once used language to his brother that would have caused an explosion had not my father (who was the only other present, and about twenty years

his senior) quickly said, "Oh, never mind your brother; he thinks that we are only two of his bairns he is speaking to " ; and adroitly turned the conversation into another channel. He was asked next day by the dominie how he could have spoken of him in the way he did; when he replied, that it was to preserve the peace when an insult (however unintentional) had been shown to his brother, in his own house. And there the matter ended. His unsatisfied ambition as to a church, and his gay and more or less expensive habits, doubtless made him occasionally capricious in his temper while in school; but he was never cruel or partial in his discipline. In school he was obeyed absolutely, not so much from a fear of punishment as from the respect in which he was held by his scholars, who would never think of making disparaging remarks in regard to him anywhere. And this feeling prevented harshness or cruelty. His being a standing candidate for a church doubtless threw around him an atmosphere which children were not capable of understanding, however much they might have been influenced by it. In society he was pleasant and even jocular, yet with a dignity that was unquestionable; but he could never throw off the dominie completely while following the calling of one. He was considered a good Greek and Latin scholar, and in every sense of the word an excellent teacher ; and the mention of his name was always responded to with respect, and at least an absence of ill-feeling on the part of those who did not sympathize with his convivial habits, which, however, did not exceed those of thoroughly respectable people in the place. In 1835 he began to teach French, which he must have learned without the assistance of others, for he sadly mangled the pronunciation of the words, as I afterwards experienced.

I dare say I was the subject of his discipline, in one form or other, more than most of the boys at the school; yet I can recall but two instances of it, towards the time when I left it. One day I was casting the rays of the sun through the school-room, by means of a piece of glass, when I was called up and told to "hold out my hand." On another occasion I was raising and letting fall the palms of my hands on my ears, for the peculiar sound it yielded by the hum of the school, when I was called up for a similar purpose. One day he was visiting our house, when I ran and hid myself from him, merely through sheepishness, owing to our seldom seeing strangers at home, and I did not present myself; in consequence of which I felt rather uneasy as to the morrow. And the trouble came, for he called me, and as I caught his eye he tossed his tawse into the middle of the floor; the meaning of which I well knew. On receiving these from me, he proceeded with his accusation and punishment before I could open my mouth, although I had nothing to say in my defense. "What made you run away from me when I was at your father's last night? Hold up your hand, sir!" This I considered "abusing his office," but I entertained no hard feelings in consequence. The only case that I remember of what might be considered cruelty, or the appearance of it, was that of a boy whom he made to stand on one foot: but he was such an odd-looking boy, and had such strange ways, that any one naturally felt a disposition to tease him. The day before Lammas Fair, in August, 1835, he gave me, for being at the top of the class, a sixpence, out of which I was to give a penny to "the girl next me." This phrase stuck in my memory, from which I conclude (although I do not remember it as a fact) that in some of the classes at least the boys and girls took their places, although the girls occupied the end of the school to the left as it was entered. It was a pity the teacher did not give me the whole

sixpence, and the girl a penny, or that some one had not "lent me a penny" for the occasion; for when the sixpence was broken, half of the remaining fivepence was spent before I got home, late at night. There was a "go-round" on the High Street, and in anticipation of the horse-race on the following day, I rode three heats on horseback, costing $1\frac{1}{2}$d.; another penny I spent on something else, and I had only $2\frac{1}{2}$d. for the fair.

On one occasion a son of his bosom friend the farmer, another boy whose father I think worked in a mill, and I were ordered to the porch. Being "sent to the porch" was a capital punishment. We were three boys that were in the same class, and hardly ever apart. We had doubtless been doing something, but I do not remember what it was. "To the porch, and lock the outer door, and make ready," was the order, which we instantly obeyed, to the astonishment and horror of the whole school. This was a punishment I never saw administered, or knew of any one who had been the subject of it. It was at least a tradition which most of the scholars understood; and it served an excellent purpose. We entered the porch, which was the ground floor of the little tower in front of the school. Feeling instinctively that something had to be done, and that immediately, I locked the only outer door in use, which added to the distress of the other boys, who, weeping bitterly, asked me, "What does he want us to do?" I explained matters, and, showing an example, urged them to do their duty, as we would get off all the easier. I had seen how the other scholars looked as they saw us going to the porch; but I could only imagine how they felt as they saw the teacher follow, tawse in hand, shortly afterwards. I dare say they expected to hear a noise something like the killing of pigs as the teacher closed the school-door which led to the porch. But he found us so abjectly submissive, and such weeping on the part of the other boys, and such lugubrious appearance of it on mine, that he said he would forgive us that time ; and told us to follow him as soon as we could into the school. We were miserable urchins, between eight and nine years old at the most; not much better than three mice in the presence of a cat. We re-entered the school, not as heroes, but pardoned criminals, and slunk away to our seats. We were all questioned by the other boys, but it was only myself that had much to say on the subject ; the other boys being averse to tell anything. I told everything, and dwelt on the other boys weeping so bitterly.

I always looked upon this event as a piece of strategy on the part of the teacher to maintain the discipline of one who was " not to be trifled with "; and it certainly had that effect. As I have said, I do not remember what was the occasion of it; but I am certain that none of us had done anything deserving of being " sent to the porch." The fact of two of the boys being the children of his most intimate friends, doubtless had some share in the strategy practised, as if it were to show that there would be no mercy for the children of poorer parents if they made themselves amenable to his discipline.

The teacher, as was the rule in parish schools, had a free house and "coal and candle," and a fixed salary, and was allowed to charge fees. The fees were dispensed with on the part of a few poor boys, who gave the teacher services in lieu thereof, such as were connected with his garden and pony. On one occasion I had remained with three of these boys to assist in carrying in his hay, when I was missed and sent for. I was a little troubled for the consequences, but on entering the school I was merely sent to my seat, with the remark, that when he wished me to carry in his hay he would ask me to do it. He had a pony which was

a great rearer ; and it was always a subject of interest to see him mount it, and *master* the most troublesome creature he had under his charge.

This was the parish school, and the best in the place. It was attended by the children of every kind of people in or near the town. As I have already said, there were no distinctions observed among the children in the school, or in ordinary out-door associations, although these would still show themselves on occasions. Thus when a gardener to a nobleman and his wife—both of them very presentable people in their way—brought their first "hopeful" to the school, some of the other children ungraciously exclaimed, "What right has a gardener's son to be dressed in that way ? " alluding to a little boy, pretty in appearance, and as prettily dressed. Sometimes the farmer's son would give the pilot's son a bloody nose; and again the quarryman's son would do the same to the farmer's son, or "send him home to his mother with his eyes beautifully coloured." Probably half of the boys attending the school went barefooted during the summer, and the other half without stockings, or what was called "slipshod." Meeting my father one day with my shoes in my hand, he sharply told me to put them on, saying that I might go barefooted when he could not afford me shoes. Dispensing with stockings during the summer was convenient for crossing the narrow entrance of the harbour at low water, in going to or returning from school, instead of taking the much longer way around the bay, towards the west. I had only to take off my shoes when passing the shallow channel, and put them on after arriving at the other side. About half of the boys had pocket-handkerchiefs ; the rest used their jacket-sleeves. Several had neither caps nor shoes during the summer, just as if they had been colts.

I was told at home that for the

first year I attended school I was never out of hot water with the other boys; which was doubtless an exaggeration. Still, there might have been some truth in what was said, for most of such affairs would present no salient points by which they could be remembered. I recollect having been badly cut up by a butcher boy, in his shirt-sleeves and with a basket on his arm. It was opposite the first house (a little old-fashioned cottage) in the town on the left on entering it from the south. It was in going to school that made the encounter so disagreeable; had it been when I was returning, I could have attended to myself. As it was, I was much indebted to an oldish man and his wife coming out of the cottage and making me presentable for the school; but I would have felt much more so had they taken me into the house, and used some kind of crockery, rather than carried a bucket of water to me in the middle of the road. From their son I got a geranium, which went by his name as long as it lived.

Opposite the back of the school resided the father of a celebrated missionary. My father's desk in the Custom-house was immediately opposite his. He dwelt at first on the top floor of a red-tiled house, to which he had access by an outside stair; but he afterwards built a one-storied house adjoining. No doubt the family. must have been many times annoyed by the boys, for that is unavoidable when people live so near a public school, however great the care to the contrary. Shortly after taking up their residence in the new building, a stone was thrown through one of its windows; which, as I have already said, was a capital offense. No sooner was the sound of the breakage heard than the boys instinctively ceased from their play, and stared at the door of the house to see who would issue from it. And out came the mistress of the family, with the fierce demand as to who

threw the stone. One boy said, "The boy Simpson." She instantly replied, with great sharpness, "Mr. Simson's son of the Ness?" (referring to me). "No," said another boy, "the boy Simpson of the Shore"; when she retreated abruptly into the house, and slammed the door after her. This was a piece of gossip, to the relating of which I found every one at home, even including my father, a ready listener. I believe I did justice to it when I compared the lady to a "raging bear" in coming to the door, and returning so abruptly after her question had been answered. "Ah!" said my mother, with a smile, "she thought she had my laddie in a snapper." I would indeed have been in a "snapper" had I thrown the unlucky stone.

The minister of the parish was a large, heavily-built and aged man that had been settled there for nearly fifty years. His predecessor filled the charge for nearly the same length of time. Both being what were called "Moderates," it was said that the parish had "lain in weeds" for a century. I recollect a squabble between him and his heritors about the canopy of his pulpit not being safe, and his refusing to preach till it was made secure. The church was in consequence closed for one Sunday at least; on which occasion I think it was that the schoolmaster preached at Dalgety, as mentioned, when a good many of the parishioners went to hear him. The canopy was then propped up by unpainted wooden beams, and afterwards taken down. I remember that the precentor showed a wonderfully big mouth when he sang. On one occasion I saw him asleep when he was wanted to begin the tune; and the clergyman doing his best to awaken him by reaching down to him with his hand, but failing in that he lengthened his reach by adding his psalm-book. Feeling that on his head, the precentor started up in astonishment, and took a little time in assuming his place in the services. The minister's son, who went to India as a chemist, used to go about botanizing on the peninsula and in the neighbourhood. He wrote the scientific part of his father's description of the parish for the Statistical Account of Scotland. He was a tall man (the length mostly in the legs), with long dark hair, and a sharp nose, with glasses on it. He generally carried a large spy-glass on his expeditions. On going to school I noticed the glass, and directed my youngest sister's attention to it. She instantly sprang for it, and reached it before me; and took it into the manse, while I waited outside to share the reward which we expected in the form of gooseberries, that were plentiful in the garden. She got a handsome reward in gooseberries, and gave the half of them to a girl with her, whom we did not meet till after finding the glass; and I got nothing, being "out" with her at the time.

Having said that the parish had been in charge of "Moderates" for nearly a century, it followed that the religious instruction of the people became a home matter. That in our house was mainly in the hands of our mother. I still retain the impression left on my mind by her teaching. It manifested itself, in a striking and indelible degree, on the occasion of the death of both grandmothers, in the spring of 1835, as I was on my way home from school, and was passing from the chemical works towards the ruined houses mentioned, during a very high tide, and as I arrived opposite a hawthorn bush inside of the stone fence there.

The Reverend Ebenezer Brown was then living at Inverkeithing. He was held in such veneration that even the children would advance near to the middle of the road and take off their caps to him as he passed. I once did that, when the person driving him—from whom different things could have been expected—laughed at me; and I never repeated the salutation. This did not prevent me from admiring his manse, or rather what was in front of it, for it had a brier-like growth almost covering the whole of it, nearly packed with sparrows' nests, which were plain to the eye—a pretty sight to almost any child. There were many such under the eaves of the Lazaretto, and in the ivy outside, but they were hidden from view.

In so small a place as Inverkeithing there were certain local offices of a social nature which my father could not well escape from filling, when called upon to do it, although he had no taste for the work. A regard for his family also doubtless led him to comply with the popular request. Thus he was instrumental in bringing to the place a dancing-master, who was assisted by his sons; one of them a dancing-master and fiddler, and the other a "sailor and fiddler," who furnished the music. They were very successful and became well liked; but unfortunately the old man at the end of the term ran away with the wife of the man in whose house they had lodged; and the sons would never again show their faces in the town. They had also classes in the neighbourhood; Limekilns, about four miles off, being one of them. On visiting an uncle of my father, at that place, with my mother, we were told that the dancing-master was coming to tea; and to our surprise he turned out to be the "sailor and fiddler" mentioned. As he was going in our direction, he could not do less than convoy us, and he gave my mother his arm; with which I was highly satisfied, as I walked alongside of them. But there was a terrible explosion after we reached home, for which I was probably to blame. "That wife of his should take the arm of a dancing-master—of a dancing-master's fiddler!" The circumstances which I have stated immediately allayed the trouble.

The dancing-master for the following year (1835), whose school I attended, was a fine-looking man; young, tall, rather slender but handsome, with fine black curly hair and bushy whiskers, and a "white choker." I think he was an Englishman, which impression was confirmed by his sending his scholars to his lodgings (opposite the woman's school which I once attended) for porter, which would appear in a white jug of good size and well filled. He certainly had a difficulty in understanding much of what some of his scholars said; none of whom indeed could *speak* English, however well they could read and understand it. I recollect one particular instance, when he asked a girl—almost too small to have been a scholar—what her name was; and she replied, "Aggy Sandy." "What does she say?" was his blank appeal to another girl, after twice asking the question. "Agnes Alexander, sir." "Oh, yes," he replied, "Agnes Alexander." This man could not have been a Scotchman, although his name was common enough in Scotland.

The night before the ball, which was to close the dancing-school, the boy who sneered so bitterly at me for having my sister's old shoes on my feet, asked me to bring, in the morning, all the flowers I could get at home to decorate the room for the occasion. A request from a boy like him was in reality a command; and it caused me some concern, for we had no flowers at home that I could fall back on. As I have already mentioned this boy twice, I will describe him. He was three, if not four, years older than myself. His usual dress was dark corduroy trousers, blue cloth jacket, with sailor's pockets outside, blue cloth cap, and loose black silk handkerchief under a folded-over collar. Figure not straight; features not refined, but agreeable; eyes light blue; hair tow-like, and a little curly; and complexion of the same shade as the hair, with no red in it, but healthy. He was restless in his movements, as if he would break away, or would sway from side to side, anything, in short, but stand still; and he had a peculiar way of winking his eyes, and spitting, almost frothing, out his words, which would come thick and close together. He was a good scholar, and an excellent hand at mental arithmetic; and his good-nature was only exceeded by his habit of sneering. His running for the teacher's porter was in keeping with his request for flowers to decorate his school; for he must be captain or master of ceremonies on all the occasions he could make himself such.

I have said that we had no flowers at home for the purpose wanted. Behind the house there was a small flower-bed, of about fifteen feet by four, cultivated by my eldest sister, but it contained nothing that would suit. The only other thing was a honey-suckle hanging from a tree. The flowers inside of the Lazaretto wall were limited to crocuses and lilies, which we used to admire as they came out in the spring, but they had long since disappeared. On thinking over the subject on my way home, I remembered that there was a rose-bush, the last remains of a garden, behind the old Cruicks' farm-house, which was then unoccupied; and on my return in the morning I picked three or four very fine white roses, which, to my relief, were accepted by "the captain and master of ceremonies," as my contribution to the decoration, although I did not tell him where I got them. And that reminds me that the ball came off pretty early in the season, or that Dr. Knox did not take up his quarters in the old house till pretty late, or that there was a very short interval between the two; for I certainly did not pick the roses while *he* was there; his name being a sufficient protection for anything in his neighbourhood.

After a few dances, three of the smallest boys at the school, including myself (who was the smallest of all), asked to go out; and on going down stairs we noticed that the floor below the ball-room was filled with small tables, all of which seemed occupied by men drinking toddy, while there was not a man to be seen above. We lingered at the door, and were called in and treated. Having a day or two before, while at the horse-race, admired the jockey and envied his horse as he poured brandy down its throat after a heat, I suppose I must have emptied a glass of toddy in the same manner. Shortly after getting into the open air we began, in a small way, and in the immediate neighbourhood, to "raise the town," when the town-officer made his appearance from the lowest floor of the building in which the drinking and dancing were going on. I was taken up-stairs, in spite of some resistance, to my mother, and there "put in quarantine" by being "lashed alongside" of her. I vehemently asked, "What had I done; what had I done?" when the officer replied that he had found me "chasing cats around the cross and making a noise," which was doubtless a "breach of the peace" at that time of night.

It was a subject of no small mortification to find myself where I was, pointed and jeered at by the girls, among whom I was, and by the boys on the opposite side of the room; and I had no friendly feeling for the "blue-eyed, florid-faced, and bald-headed blockhead" that had done the mischief. I was perfectly sensible of everything, but irritable, and not so observant as I might otherwise have been; while what I had previously noticed became somewhat loosened and muddled in my memory. Some of the men must have made their appearance in the ball-room; but I do not recollect that any of them left their toddy on the floor below, where their hearts seemed to be. It was a children's dancing-school ball, and the dancing seems to have been confined to them. Had all of the four "gay"

people" spoken of been living in the town it might have been otherwise; but the gallant young doctor who married the widow, and the fashionable young wife of the old man had left it; and there were apparently no others to take their places. I had not noticed who were drinking below, for I did not get beyond the table next the door, and was too much engrossed while there to think of anything else; and I had no chance of looking in while being taken up-stairs by the officer. But I presume the new superintendent of quarantine would be among the drinkers, for his wife and three daughters were in the ball-room. Being a recently arrived Englishman, he may have preferred something else to toddy; his choice being rum and brandy, with which he "fortified" his tea and coffee. He did not seem to be popular at first; perhaps from some feeling of disparagement of "Scotch bodies, and Fife at that," or like a foolish person who said that while he lived there he would have an "opportunity for wearing out his old clothes." His boisterous ways soon procured him a nickname. As I have already said, his two daughters by his first wife were at the ball; interesting and attractive girls, approaching womanhood, who were shortly afterwards lost on the coast of India. There were also his "little angel," his second wife, and her little angel, who made considerable fun of me, but for which I did not blame her.

This English family made an interesting addition to the limited society of the place, such as it was, and added to the importance of the Captain's commission as a passport for him to go anywhere. They took up their residence in the wretched old farm-house above the Ferry, on the old road over the hills; a building which seems to have been erected when agriculture there was at a low ebb. At that time there must have been few dwellings in the village that could be rented to accommodate newly-arrived people of their standing.

There were two old maiden sisters who lived opposite the end of the school play-ground, in a small red-tiled house with a tall chimney. One of them, who was of a fair complexion and delicate, almost lived at the window, "flowering" on what seemed an endless web; and, as she said, had never seen Preston Crescent since a house had been built on it. The other sister, a small, dark-featured, hardy and active woman, did all kinds of jobs in private families on special occasions, or anything by which she could scrape together an honest living. At the window there were little things for sale, suitable for children. It was in this house that, for several years before we left Inverkeithing, we ate our "pieces" at mid-day when at school, or between sermons on Sunday, and used it generally as a place of call or convenience; and for which ample remuneration was made. There were several other families residing at a distance that made a similar use of the house. This was a great place for certain kinds of gossip that was circumstantial and reliable; and we all enjoyed it thoroughly. The old maid at the window collected the gossip that was brought into the house, while the other one ferreted outside for it in every direction. It was in this house that my eldest and youngest sisters caught typhus fever, from a girl of the place recently recovered from it coming into the house, among so many children, sooner than was consistent with safety. They soon got over the illness; but the third boy of the family caught it, as the other two were recovering; and it developed into typhus in its most malignant form, but from which he recovered.

At this time there was a large distillery in Inverkeithing, in full operation, which required an attendance of two excisemen. I remember three of them, all apparently past middle life. Judging by my observation of this class of men elsewhere and afterwards, I would describe these excisemen as rather superior men; probably young military or naval officers, who had been discharged at the peace of 1815, or the children of others who had been killed in the service. They certainly were in every way superior to what I afterwards met under the name of gaugers in a large community. Cheap rents and the absence of social pressure, in a small population, enabled the excisemen, with the king's commission in their pockets, to hold up their heads before the world.

One of these excisemen and his wife had in every way a highly presentable appearance; but I could judge more accurately of their two boys, who attended the school—one of about ten and the other of about thirteen years. I do not remember seeing boys at any school that were more creditable in their appearance, dress, manners, and behaviour. Another exciseman and his wife, both well up in years, presented a plainer appearance than those alluded to, and rather old-fashioned, but very respectable-looking withal. They occupied part of the teacher's pew in the parish church, immediately in front of ours. Having the teacher so near me all the year round—Sundays and Saturdays alike—was not to my liking; but the case was made worse by the exciseman's only child, a girl a little older than myself, and of a very pert disposition. She would watch me during the service, and especially to see whether I was looking on the book and joining in the singing of the psalms. She managed to keep me in every way in order, to appearance at least, even if she had to thrust her straw bonnet, containing blue eyes and a scarlet countenance, over the back of her seat for that purpose. I had no redress but to say to myself that she was a "nasty little puggie"; the last of which words became her nickname at the school.

Another of these excisemen was a tall, white-haired, venerable-looking man, who had been reduced from the position of a supervisor, in consequence of his having accepted a small keg of whiskey from a person who turned round and informed on him. The whiskey was received under the most honourable of circumstances, with the single exception, that such presents were prohibited under *any* circumstances. His wife, considerably past middle life, was a Highland lady, not far removed from the main stem of a clan. She was tall and stout, and had blue eyes, dark brown hair, and a very dark florid complexion. Dressed in black and a cap or head-gear of what looked like dark-brown flowered lace, and with her dignified air and Highland spirit, she presented an imposing appearance. I was brought much in contact with her. What surprised and disappointed me was that, although she was large enough to make two mothers of a little boy like me, I never saw any children about the house for me to play with. She had a great fancy for blackbirds; and as these were very plentiful about the Lazaretto, I got them for her. But she was very particular about the kind she wanted; it was *whistlers* I was to bring, and did I know which were the whistlers? "Oh, yes, ma'am," I said, "I know which are the whistlers." I remember how sorry I felt on losing a young whistler as I was taking it to her, while on my way to school, by trying its power of flight and never recovering it. To me she appeared so much of a gentlemanly lady that I thought she must have whistled herself. She certainly swore a little, on one occasion at least, when she went down-stairs to visit her kitchen, to see who was the visitor there, and opened the door of her maid's closet-bed and found a man in his dirty shoes standing on her "good bed-clothes." My father was very intimate with her, and many a good-natured bout they had on the Highland and Lowland questions. My father would, in the best of humour, use such expressions as "half-savage, half-barbarous, blood-thirsty clans," and speak of "monkeys being dressed in tartan"; when she would retort, in as good humour, but what she said I do not remember, except that she would occasionally drop words that were not used in our house.

Years afterwards, when she was advanced in life, I had occasion to convoy this lady to friends in Edinburgh, whom she was visiting. A little ahead of us I saw a number of soldiers walking in the opposite direction, late at night, apparently drunk and disorderly. With her on my arm, I abruptly left the narrow sidewalk for the middle of the street; which so mortified the soldiers that they instantly made room for several like us to pass. I felt sorry for what I had done on finding that the poor fellows were not so far "on" as I thought. I also apologized to the lady, saying that I thought it best to err on the safe side under the circumstances; when she incidentally replied, "Oh, yes, I am a great coward at night, but I'll face the devil in daylight!"

My father was drafted from the Customs to act as superintendent of quarantine, but in what particular year I am uncertain. I see that he is officially designated by the latter office on the 25th May, 1829; but his appointment was certainly made years before that. When the cholera in 1832 disappeared, the use of the Lazaretto, as I have already said, was at an end. What little occasion there was for quarantine purposes could be met by the remaining hulk or guardship in St. Margaret's Hope, which fell to the charge of a naval officer; the first one employed being the one I have referred to. While the superintendent, my father was requested by the authorities at headquarters to recommend a local surgeon to act during the cholera; and the gallant young doctor referred to received the appointment. The fee, it was said, was a guinea a ship, which yielded five hundred guineas. This, it was alleged, was spent by the doctor in paying his debts and removing, some time afterwards, to a Colony. When the merchant vessels were riding quarantine in St. Margaret's Hope, the farmers and others on both sides of the firth suffered considerably by boats' crews, in spite of the quarantine regulations, exercising "free pratique" with the shore at night, and plundering everything green which they could eat. Once a vessel, in spite of her "clean bill of health," was refused admittance to Leith by the tide surveyor, for the reason of an extraordinary blackness which he accidentally discovered in the mouth of one of the boys on board. The case was referred to the doctor, who replied that there was no danger; and that the boy only required to be fed on porridge and turnips.

For the education and general advantage of his large family, my father applied to the Board of Customs to be removed to Leith; where, I believe, he accepted a lower position in point of rank, but having a larger salary attached to it. And so, in September or October, 1835, we left Inverkeithing.

Inverkeithing is a very ancient town, that at one time, it is said, took precedence of Edinburgh in the convention of royal burghs. It is within nine or ten miles of that city as the crow flies, but is hardly (if at all) observable from the steamer while on its way to Stirling. The vessel on turning the projecting point of the Earl of Rosebery's grounds, on the south, keeps nearly on a straight line till it arrives at the North Queensferry. Between these two points, St. Davids shows itself on the opposite side of the firth; and within a mile towards the west is Inverkeithing, prettily situated on a bay of the same name, with a narrow entrance, formed by the East and West Nesses that almost hide the town from view. It may, for that reason, be said to be, in a sense, "out of the world," particularly after a ferry was established at Granton, which took away the traffic, such as it was, that passed between the North and South Queensferries, and when mails and travellers were carried by rail, and in the absence, till lately, of any railway in the neighbourhood.

Notwithstanding that the dignified "ancient burgh" thus became (what it was pretty much always) a sleepy little place, out of sight and almost out of mind, we could still have expected that such an important work as the *Encyclopædia Britannica* would have been more accurate in its description of it than to have said that "it is beautifully situated on the brow of an acclivity rising from the margin of a bay called St. Margaret's Hope." Had Inverkeithing been situated in some secluded nook on the coast of Japan, in place of within sight of Edinburgh, the bay on the edge of which it is built could not have been more incorrectly described. St. Margaret's Hope is between one and two miles by land from Inverkeithing, and several miles by water, judging from where it is supposed to begin. It may be said to extend from somewhere above the North and South Queensferries to the west, as far as there is deep water with good anchorage. Thus the five or six quarantine hulks rode at anchor probably opposite Rosyth burying-ground, pretty close together, yet scattering, with room to swing with the wind and tide. The remaining hulk, when I saw it from the hamlet of Rosyth, as already mentioned, stood out in the firth at an angle that would bring it nearly opposite the burying-ground mentioned.

Chambers' *Gazetteer of Scotland* (published in 1846) is also inaccurate in regard to St. Margaret's Hope, for it says that "the bay between the promontory and Rosyth Castle is called St. Margaret's Hope." That in reality is St. Margaret's Bay; a little bight that for the most part goes dry at low water, and extends for a short distance to a grassy point called Limpet Ness. This was the most convenient spot for Queen Margaret to land, on her way to Dunfermline, when the wind was from the east; for her vessel had only to drive past the North Queensferry, and take a sharp turn to the right, and enter the refuge prepared for it by nature.

Inverkeithing, when I left it in 1835, had, as I have already said, a large distillery in operation; but it was discontinued some time before 1841. The chemical works were closed in 1833 or 1834, in consequence of the death of their owner. There were salt-pans in use up to 1835, so far as I remember. These had a well built of stone to hold the salt water, apparently of recent or modern construction, judging from the style of the work; between which and a foundery, a bone-mill and a ship-building yard was a public road. This well was not railed or fenced off, so that there was much danger in passing it at night, in the absence of lamps so far as I recollect. The salt-pans, immediately back of the well, and rising with the ground, seemed to be of wood, and presented a wretched appearance, and as if covered with soot. I recollect how peculiar a noise was made by the "salters" when pumping the water from the well for the purpose of converting it into salt by boiling. Chambers, in 1846, alludes to "three public works on an extensive scale, namely, a distillery, a magnesia work, and some salt-pans"—the first two at least having been long out of use. Chambers is much more out of his reckoning when he says: — "The

port of Inverkeithing is, by authority, a place for vessels riding quarantine, and for that purpose Government stations a body of officers, with a lazaretto on shore"; for, as I have already stated, the Lazaretto was discontinued shortly after 1832, and sold in 1835.

Besides the works mentioned, there were a small tannery and meal or flour mill, opposite each other, on the town-side of a bridge that crossed what could hardly be called a stream, although the tide, I think, reached that far;* and further up, on the opposite side of it, and "out of town," was a small fire-clay brick work. The only other work was a small ropery on the crescent that led to the East Ness.

Small as Inverkeithing was, it had a provost and twelve councillors, a town-clerk, and a town-officer; in consequence of which it was doubtless well governed, if the number of those in "authority" would ensure that.

I do not remember anything particularly exciting in the town excepting at Lammas fair and its horse race, to which I have already alluded. Every one, for miles around, made a public appearance on that day, and entered into the spirit of it. Even the herds had a half-holiday; in anticipation of which they carefully kept their cows off a piece of grass long in advance of the fair (and hence called a "Lammas bite"), so that on the morning of it the animals were turned into the reserve pasture, which would furnish them as much grass during the forenoon as they could get the whole day under or-

* At this time there was no obstruction to the flow of the fresh water till nearly opposite the distillery, where there was a dam with the usual sluice. In time of floods the stream would overflow the bank, on the right, and lodge where there was a row of willow trees, at the bottom of some gardens, one of which belonged to the owner of the tannery, and contained an ancient stone dove-cot.

dinary circumstances. I always took an interest in the herds' "Lammas bites." All that took place at the fair was merry-making and treating each other, at the stands in the principal part of the main (or only) street, with gingerbread and such things ; which was called a "fairin'."

The semi-annual or periodical sale of oxen, fed on the refuse of the distillery, was also an event in the place, especially as some of the animals, on being removed by the purchasers, would become "raised" or go wild, and cause a disturbance in the neighbourhood. Another excitement proper to the place was the launch of a vessel. That was always a gala day, which was looked forward to with much interest long before its occurrence, and called forth a full assembly of spectators. The last two vessels which I saw launched was a brig, of about 200 tons, called the *Lord Dalmeny*, and a sloop, called the *Esperance*, that had a peculiarly square stern, and was commanded by "Handy Davie" (from having lost a hand), a relative, I believe, of the builder. The first I may say I saw built, from the keel upwards, but I regretted that I could not get on board of her when she was launched, although I made a "mess of myself" on the greased ways immediately afterwards. I might also say that I saw her rigged, and was on board of her every Sunday between sermons ; but I lost conceit of her, large as I thought she was, on seeing her very soon thereafter discharging coals at the coal-hill of Leith. The *Esperance* was laid down inside of the *Lord Dalmeny* while she was being built, and was launched before her. I could not learn when the launch was to take place, but I saw it, notwithstanding, from immediately behind our house, a little to the right, and well on in the evening, when I heard the sound of the mallets raising her on the ways, and the huzzaing as she entered the water, in a direction almost on a line with the blacksmith's shop, which was immediately to the left of the chemical works. A very short time elapsed between the first sound of the mallets and the vessel entering the bay. I particularly remember the *Esperance*, for she came alongside of the pier at the Lazaretto and took on board our furniture for Leith; which I saw packed, or braced, as already mentioned, and shipped. It was after the dismissal of the school for the vacations; towards the latter end of which I found time hang so heavily on my hands, at our isolated residence, that I was glad— as the phrase ran—to find "any kind of a hole to put my head into." I spent my time in looking after things, as if I had been placed there to see that the man employed did his work ; which was not "with all his might," but steadily, while he took many a snuff when at it. He might even have thought that I was there to watch him, if the work had been done on "days' wages."

Inverkeithing, at the time alluded to, being on the way of certain kinds of traffic between the north and the south, had its share of all kinds of native and foreign "gangrel bodies" passing through it. The latter included Swiss girls with tambourine and singing, "Buy a broom," which was of wood shaved off the stick of which it was made. There were also "bearded blackguards" with monkeys, raccoons and bears. The dancing bears attracted my particular attention, from the Bible story of two she ones coming out of a wood and tearing forty-and-two children for mocking the prophet by saying, "Go up, thou bald-head." The allusion had reference to my feeling for old Daniel Nicol, and his cat destroying my rabbits inside of the Lazaretto wall, as already mentioned (p. 9). The place was well suited for a rabbit-warren on a small scale ; and what with the grass inside of it, and the feed which I could otherwise find, I imagined I could make the business profitable even by selling rabbits a month old at fourpence a pair ; but, as I have already said, " Every young rabbit, whether tame or wild, put into the enclosure disappeared, nor could a brood be reared; the old rabbits only held their own" (p. 10). I might have even cursed the old man and his cat. Daniel was certainly not a prophet; but I could not say whether he was or was not a "bald-head," for often as I was in his house it was almost always when he was out ; and he had a habit of wearing his blue bonnet wherever he was, and might have slept with it on his head for anything I knew to the contrary. The bear for the reason mentioned appeared to me as partaking something of a "person"; which impression was increased by its dancing acquirements, its size, and the muzzle that it had on it. Moreover, it was a wild animal that could not be handled or approached, while I had a crude idea of the relation that such "strange brutes" bore to the human family. It was always a subject of interest where the bears were lodged, and on what they were fed — sheeps' heads or what not. Every such bear I convoyed out of the town when the time of its leaving it was at all suitable. One on leaving it in our direction began vigorously to dig into a "bum-bee's bink" at the witches' knowe, disregardless of the attack of the bees, while its owners were refreshing themselves and counting their coppers ; and it was then I learned that it had a great taste for honey. On another occasion, when I was not present, a bear left the town in the opposite direction, when a tollman of a surly disposition insisted on a fare for it, and swung his gate to on its master refusing to pay it. The "bearded blackguard" immediately drew the bear to him and threatened to unmuzzle it, to "fight its way through," if a passage was not given; which the tollman was glad to assent to. I asked again and again to have

the scene described to me, and envied the boy who was present at a squabble of that kind.

Indeed in a place like Inverkeithing the most trifling thing became a subject of more or less interest. Even a journeyman tailor from Edinburgh taking up his residence in it became the town's talk, as to how he would succeed, and who would "patronize" him. — Occasionally a regiment or several companies of foot-soldiers would be billeted in the town on their way towards the south, and answer the roll-call and have their ranks dressed in the morning. —Frequently would droves of cattle pass through it on their way from the north. These would sometimes have their front feet shod to enable them to stand the travelling.—The examination of the parish school was always an event in the place ; but it was exceeded by the sacrament in the parish church, on which occasion there would be present people that were hardly ever seen inside of it at other times.—I particularly recollect an excitement caused by a trial at the town-house of several "big blackguard boys" for annoying the children of several families while on their way to and from school ; and of their parents paying a heavy fine rather than let them go to jail, which effectually stopped that trouble.—Laying the foundation of a building was a matter of no small importance in the place. Three of these I particularly remember. The first was that of the provost, who was a grocer, building a shop, and a house over it, immediately opposite the opening that led to the cross, and on ground that had been occupied by some miserable old houses, one of which was entered by an outside stair, and in which dwelt a crooked, lame and limping woman that lived by begging and selling "spunks"— that is, splints of wood dipped in brimstone, and used in connection with a tinder-box and flint and steel, for at this time a lucifer-match was not to be seen in the place. Another building was the corn market, which was erected on an open spot that was covered by nettles and rubbish; which also covered the ground in front of the place on which the house behind the school-house to which I have alluded (p. 39) was built.—The return of an Inverkeithing man from the East Indies, with a coloured wife and a large family of children, all born there, and a corresponding establishment of servants, or rather slaves, was quite an event in the social history of the place. At first the children attended the parish school, but afterwards had a tutor, which created a sensation.

I have no recollection of political or municipal squabbles, although there were doubtless such; nor of social meetings among the people generally beyond a dim remembrance of feasting, in the way of dinners and suppers, and especially suppers, and the invariable toddy drinking, which was not apparently carried to excess as a rule. Indeed in such a place people could have few sources of amusement after business hours but gossip and tea and toddy. In all probability few newspapers would be taken; but these would doubtless be well read by the little circles subscribing for them. There was a town library, contained in a bookcase standing against the upper end of the school-room, towards the left. I saw it opened but once. The binding of the books indicated that they were standard or old-fashioned works. — Sometimes, but not very often, there would be a children's party, or something like it; on which occasions our maid would be sent to bring us home; and she would have some one to see *her* home; so that in passing, in the dark, the uninhabited old Cruicks' farm-house, and the ruinous houses below it, near the edge of the bay, we would feel secure when in the presence of two grown-up people.

Inverkeithing had but one main street, which separated into two, a little before the parish church was reached, on entering it from the south; the left-hand branch going north, and the right-hand one east down the mill wynd. This division formed a triangle, the base of which was the road back of the church and parish school that led to the entrance to the harbour wynd. The other wynd led to Dunfermline. Opposite the school-house was a vennel—that is, a small and narrow street with no outlet. There were several narrow closes, running in the direction of the harbour; but I never went down any of them except to go to the old weaver to get my hair cut, as mentioned (p. 17). His door was the first or second one from the entrance on the left, on the ground floor; and even then I would hesitate and survey the place before entering it; for these closes had the reputation of harbouring a wild set, with which I was not desirous of coming in contact, in consequence of the fresh tradition of Burke and Hare "burking" people in such places in Edinburgh, and selling their bodies to Dr. Knox, whose summer residence in our immediate neighbourhood intensified the feeling in question. I remember that there was another wild set—the women especially—whose house was up an overhanging stair, which I think was of wood, on the left-hand side of the opening that led to the cross, going from the direction of the church. I still recollect their names.

The main, I might say the only, street in Inverkeithing had two small detached "blocks" of houses, both on the right as the town was entered from the south. The first commenced with the "beggars' inn," kept by Jenny ——, and ended where the street widened, a little before Dunfermline wynd was reached; and the other began where it narrowed, near where there was an ancient draw-well, built on the street, and opposite a tall building in ruins, called, I think, the "Gala Tower," and ended at the opening that led to the cross. The only passages from the town to the harbour were by the wynd mentioned, and by a path or road (but not a street) from the inner end of the corn market. The town, as already mentioned, had a crescent extending from the harbour proper to the East Ness, at the entrance of the bay. Only one house had a door-bell; a few (but very few) had knockers; the others had nature's provision—the tap of a stick, or a rap from the knuckles. No house had any kind of bell-hanging; nor do I think that any shop had a sign, or house a door-plate, or street a name painted on it, for in such a small place these seemed unnecessary. There were doubtless a few street lamps, burning oil, but I do not recollect that there were such. The town contained four bridges, not counting what connected the two quays at the port. These were at the harbour and mill wynds, the Boreland farm* and the brick-work. I have already alluded to a well on the beach near the foundery (p. 33) and an ancient one on the main street. There was another in a recess from the street at the "Poplars"; another behind the church-yard; and I think there was another near the road that led to the Boreland farm. The first and last two were pump-wells. There were a number of old buildings in the town, of some of which I cannot speak particularly. Opposite the church there was one called the "Ark," in which dwelt a turner, nicknamed "Noah," from whom I used to buy

---

* This bridge had a fine way connecting it with the town, and an interesting view during the summer could be had from it, looking in the direction of the mill. The ground between these was much frequented by the boys fishing for minnows, or otherwise amusing themselves, during the midday interval at school.

very superior tops at a penny apiece.

The parish church, a modern structure, was built on to a very ancient tower, which was square in shape and of a moderate height, and had a clock in it, and harboured a breed of wild pigeons in the top of it. This church was small in size, notwithstanding which its roof was supported by round stone columns, forming, I think, two rows of three pillars each. Inside of the tower was a very ancient stone font, of large size, which divided the passage into the church. While repairs were being done to the roof of the church it took fire; which formed an epoch in the history of the town, as things that happened were spoken of as having occurred during that year or in such or such a year before or after it. The school was immediately adjoining, with the church-yard and its watch-house in ruins between them, and was a handsome modern building. There was also the dissenting church of Ebenezer Brown. The object that attracted my notice the most of all was the cross. It consisted of a round pillar on the top of which was a griffin, surrounded by a low round stone wall and iron railing. This was doubtless erected on the place on which the real cross had stood.

The town was partly surrounded by three farms belonging to the Preston family — Spencerfield, the Boreland and Belle Knowes, a very valuable property, that extended from near St. Davids to the rear of the town near the Dunfermline wynd. I am uncertain whether the pretty plantation on Letham hill, which dipped towards the sea near St. Davids, belonged to the Preston estate. Next to it came the flag-staff, surrounded by a wall with a gate, to which I have already alluded. This prominent land-mark was a favourite resort for us between sermons, when the weather was suitable, for we could get a fine view of our place from it. I have been told that the flag is always hoisted on rent-days. Along the back of the town were gardens bounded by a wall, from which to near the top of the ridge were narrow strips of ground in cultivation, extending from Belle Knowes' farm to a bullet-headed hill covered with rich green grass, back of the witches knowe, and on which was a growth of wild garlic —the only place where I found it. On the side of the town reaching to the harbour there were also gardens. From the Lazaretto we had a complete view of the bay, and everything surrounding it; the most striking objects being the gardens reaching to the harbour, a very tall old-fashioned house containing deep rows of chimneys, and a row of tall Lombardy poplars, that were festooned with sparrows' nests. The manse and its garden reaching to the water completed the objects that naturally attracted the eye. There was also a strip of ground, several feet higher than the road, and covered with grass, at both ends of the town, on the left-hand side as it was entered from the south, that were called the west and east loans.

The bay of Inverkeithing is capable of being converted into an excellent harbour of some depth, if the demands of business called for it. All that would be necessary to be done would be to contract the entrance by a sea wall and insert a gate, and deepen the space inside. Under any circumstances it would be what is called a " dry harbour," for the tide recedes a considerable way beyond the entrance; but a deep-water channel could be made and doubtless maintained by scouring it with the water collected behind the gate. At the time I have alluded to, the shallow channel leading to the town passed close to the West Ness pier, and had poles indicating its course inland. The depth of water, at ordinary tides, might have admitted loaded vessels of 200 tons. The circumference of the bay consisted of the natural beach except at the town ; the harbour of which consisted of two quays opposite each other, with a small branch to the left as it was entered.

I could still enter the town and point out the residences and give the names and callings of the principal people, and of those whose actions or characters presented salient points, and describe them pretty accurately ; but it would not always be in good taste, were it only owing to the many kindnesses of which I had been the subject at the hands of most of them. I particularly recollect a couple whose family consisted only of a cat and parrot, and in whose dwelling there were troubles, but none of them of a deadly nature. The parrot had in some way learned, or been taught by others outside, to take a part in these squabbles. Frequently in passing the door I would walk as slowly as I could to hear what was passing within. The town had its full share of " characters " of various kinds; but I will allude to none of them except to a seafaring man of whom nothing good was expected, yet who recovered himself and became so industrious and enterprising as, among other things, to carry grain in an old yacht between ports in the firth, having no one on board but himself and his dog. I could still give many of the slang phrases and doggerel of the place, but these would not be always presentable.

I may be allowed to allude to a particular family. One Sunday afternoon, as I was going home from church, I took particular notice of the pigeons belonging to it—ordinary birds, but of a very pretty appearance—when the head of it said, " I see you are admiring my doos." Yes, I said, I was. " Well then," said he, " look in as you go home from school to-morrow, and I will give you a pair."* This was a tall

* There were also some "fantails," which I do not think were ever seen on the street, near as that was to the " doo-

and stout man, who owned the ground he farmed, while his wife was a little but stout-built woman, both of them well advanced in years, and in dress and appearance not unlike Quakers, although I believe they were Kirk people. Their oldest son pressed me, after my father's death, to tell him, as a favour, in what respect he had been indebted to him. I replied that he had recommended him (which I believe was equivalent to an appointment) to his government office, which he filled while attending to his business proper; and that it was entirely in keeping with his character never to have mentioned the subject to him. An unmarried daughter, of a prim and precise but lady-like appearance and disposition, had always a kind word for us. Another son went about with a dog and gun, and wore a coat containing so many "pouches" that I could never manage to count them.

The maiden sister of the principal grocer, who was the provost of the burgh, and who lived with him, used to frequent the neighbourhood of our place several days every month with her "washing," where there was a suitable piece of grass sloping to the sea, and bleach it with the water from Pinkie well, a few yards to the west. She was "a little black-eyed body," and always had a pleasant word for us when going to and from school.

There was a house, entered from the right on going down the harbour wynd, in connection with which many pleasant associations are wrapped up in my memory. It was

situated in the middle of a narrow garden, which, I think, had a door at the bottom of it. It was a red-tiled building having a wing or extension towards the water. Its occupants were a widow, well advanced in years, and almost toothless, and of a dark complexion; and an unmarried daughter, also of a swarthy hue, and of a very affected tone of voice, which had become natural to her, and was pleasant. From these two ladies I received many kindnesses.

The last change in the population of the place was a family in the spring of 1835 temporarily taking up their residence in the house opposite ours, on the other side of the entrance to the bay, and which, as I have already said (p. 25), had been long uninhabited, and had the reputation of being haunted by ghosts; in which condition it had been an eyesore to us. The father of the family had just left a factorship or some such occupation. The children were very prepossessing in every way, and, becoming as it were neighbours, helped to relieve us of the monotony of our existence in our isolated residence. The water between us kept the children good friends. We could see them at their plays, and by going to the end of our pier would call on them. When the tide was out we would cross over to them, or they to us; and we would sometimes visit them on our way home from school when the tide suited; but we had to be careful in getting over in time, or we would have had a long journey home by land.

In referring to the cholera in 1832, I have said that in regard to the subject of death I was satisfied that I was incapable of realizing it, at that time, "unless it had been of the death of an inmate of the family, or of one with whom I had stood in close and constant relationship" (p. 16). The first case that was brought home particularly to me was

cot." Among my earliest recollections is that of a very large flock of pigeons that were kept in the "small dilapidated stone building that apparently had been used as a temporary smithy," inside of the Lazaretto wall; from which they were transferred to the upper story of the Lazaretto itself, with a large sail spread on the floor, and some of the slats left open. But very soon they disappeared for the most part, in consequence of people shooting them.

that of an old man, standing in near relationship to the Inverkeithing farmer first alluded to. He generally went under the name of "Auld Pow," owing to his bald head. He was killed by the horses that were turning the threshing - mill. As may be easily imagined, there were many stories of the appearance of "Auld Pow's" ghost. Shortly after this two boys of the farmer, one about three years and the other about five years old, were scalded in the farm boiler; the youngest to above the hips, in consequence of which he died. They were pretty children, the youngest especially; fair-haired, black-eyed and almost little Spaniards in their complexion (one parent being very dark, and the other very fair) — literally "olive branches." The event created an intense feeling in the neighbourhood. The parents paid us a visit immediately thereafter, and the mother, sitting at the fireside, took the fourth boy of the family on her knee, and acted very strangely in regard to him. She said that he was exactly of the age of the child she had lost, and commenced to take off his shoes (showing a hole in one of his stockings, at the sight of which my mother winced), and burst into tears, amid the solemn silence of all present. This was the first occasion on which I saw a grown-up person weep. I remember another painful occurrence of a different nature—that of two boys, of about four or five years old, playing on a heap of sand, at the beginning of the crescent, and in some way one of them having had the sand thrown in his face, and completely covering his eye-balls.*

It remains for me to speak of the Cruicks' Peninsula. In the description given of it in the Statistical Account of Scotland, already referred

to (p. 40), I think it is stated that it is considerably above a mile across it, and that it rises to 300 feet at its highest part. The neck connecting it with what might be called the *mainland* is about half a mile in length, which might be about a fifth of its entire circumference. On the northern side of this neck is Inverkeithing bay, and on the southern is St. Margaret's bay. The old road from the direction of Inverkeithing passed between the chemical works and the blacksmith's shop, and crossed it diagonally, nearly in a straight line, till it ended at the brow of the hill above the Ferry. This peninsula occupies a peculiar position in the estuary of the Forth, and presents a striking appearance, and I believe is the only one of the kind connected with the river. The Forth ceases to be a river at or near Alloa, where it widens into the firth, and contracts between the ferries, by the jutting out of the Cruicks' peninsula; so that in looking west from it the water has almost the appearance of being a lake. The projecting ground by being turned by vessels flying from a storm from the east or west gives ample protection to them on either side of it.

The ground in my time presented nothing in the way of adornment except the recent erection of the new Cruicks' farm-house, with some trees which had not had time to grow. There was also Mr. Cathcart's house at St. Margaret's, with some pine or fir trees which had just been planted. The other place, which had a pretty appearance, I have already alluded to (p. 35) as "a recent plantation on the brow of the village" of the Ferry. This I believe belonged to a Captain Macconnochie, who, I also believe, was the well-known Captain Macconnochie of penal transportation discussion. If the whole peninsula could have become the property of a man of taste, it could have been made an attractive place, with the water surrounding it (when the

---

* The population of Inverkeithing has been going down. In 1861 it was 1,817 ; in 1871, 1,755 ; and in 1881, 1,646.

tide was in) and the various aspects of the land in immediate view.

There was nothing very striking in the appearance of the place. Behind the first ridge, facing Inverkeithing, and extending from behind the chemical works to opposite the old Cruicks' farm-house, it was generally believed that the Parliamentary army in Cromwell's time erected their batteries in the action that was fought in the neighbourhood. At the same time there had doubtless been a battery erected to guard the entrance of the bay, for about a hundred yards from it there were two sides of a square that appeared to have been the remains of a light earthwork. In Cromwell's time it would seem that there was nothing but a bridle-road across the hills, with a few houses at the Ferry, and a landing at projecting rocks. Even in my father's recollection a landing was effected at what appeared to me to be a rock, near the light-house, on the west side of the pier, and close to where it commenced. A few of the houses at the Ferry in 1835 doubtless existed in the middle of the seventeenth century; and the same might possibly be said of the black-smith's shop alluded to, and especially of the old farm-house on the hill (p. 42). In all probability the coast from the Ferry to Inverkeithing, including both sides of the entrance to the bay, was as nature left it; that is, there would be no piers before the town was reached. In my time the East Ness had no pier, but a substantial wall, of blue stone, of apparently recent construction, that served the purpose of a pier, at the sharp turn of the coast; and a low stone platform for boats at different stages of the tide. The pier at the West Ness (as seen in the frontis-piece) was apparently of considerable age, and was built, I think, of blue and sand stone.

From the first ridge on the peninsula, on the north side, the road kept ascending till it reached the second, the highest part, between Port Laing sands on the east and St. Margaret's bay on the west; both of which bend inwards, and contract the ground to its narrowest width. Between these ridges the ground dips somewhat to the west. I have already alluded to the views to be had from this part (pp. 13 and 27). Looking towards the east, we have before us both coasts of the Forth, and its islands — Inchgarvie to the right, Inchcolm to the left, Inchmickery in the centre, and beyond that, but a little to the left of it, Inchkeith, and Cramond island to the right, a little beyond Barnbougle Point. On arriving at the top of the hill behind the Ferry, the eye is immediately attracted by the view on the north coast, from the East Ness to beyond Inchcolm, which is really fine. The other views are of a less striking nature, and more or less attractive by associations of ideas, and the seasons, and the state of the atmosphere. A very interesting one, from this elevated spot, presents itself from the East Ness to the left, taking in both sides of the almost land-locked little inlet (when the tide is in), with Inverkeithing rising from the water, and the ground rising behind it, and the country still rising behind that, excepting that the row of old white-washed houses called Castland Hill, acting like an eye-sore, spoiled the view in that direction. When the Lazaretto was nearly reached, on the way from the Ferry, a view could be had of Edinburgh Castle; and at times the reports of its salutes could be heard. I have already said (p. 13) that "the Ferry Hills, east of the road," extending to Caroline's Nose (or "the Caroline Knowes," as it was frequently expressed), were "clothed throughout in the finest of pasture, and (one might say) covered with horses, cattle and sheep." Caroline's Nose, in 1835, was a perpendicular precipice which was being gradually eaten away by quarrying the stone for street-paving and such purposes. If the work has been kept up till now there must be comparatively little remaining of it. Laying the land down and keeping it so long in pasture had its origin in its having been leased by a very enterprising and successful man at the Ferry, who kept a first-class inn there, of moderate size, and was extensively connected with those having mail contracts and posting generally. Grazing the land with horses, cattle and sheep, all at the same time, kept it in the fine condition described. He seemed to have occasionally dealt in cattle, or grazed them temporarily for others, for there were many of them ; and they would sometimes become wild and break out of the enclosure, which is the reason for what I have said, that "none of us had ever thought of passing over the pasture land . . . . unless we were with a grown-up person" (p. 13).

The highest ridge which I have alluded to is nearly opposite the middle of Port Laing sands ; the eastern end being about a hundred yards from the road. It is very short in length. The western end of it looks down on St. Margaret's bay. The best view to be got, looking towards the east, is from where there was a tomb, erected by a person who apparently never occupied it. It was immediately above the sands. The prospect seems to have attracted him, as if that was to be the spot where he wished to rest. It was a plain structure, on a sharp incline, with the entrance facing the east. The top, surrounded by a low parapet, was covered with whin bushes. Everything connected with it looked as if it had never been cared for from the day of its erection. Latterly the door gave way, and nothing was to be seen inside but a dark-brown empty jar, of a large size and antique shape. This tomb was nearly in the middle of a small field-like enclosure, formed by the most common-place dry-stone dyke, in-

side of which I never saw an animal grazing.

In the preceding pages I have frequently alluded to Port Laing sands, although the expression generally made use of was "Pork Laing." It was a place considerably spoken of, as it was the only sandy beach within miles on either side of it. In my time, with the pasture land above it, it was a pretty place, not merely in a child's estimation, but in that of any one. It was about half a mile from our house, a little beyond "Henderson's dyke," a dry-stone fence that ran from the sea towards the walled garden of the Cruicks' farm-house, and met another such fence that led to the sea inside of the bay. These and the sea coast formed nearly a square, and constituted "the limits" (pp. 8, 15 and 23) inside of which we felt that no one but ourselves and friends and the farmer's people had a right to enter. Immediately after passing Henderson's dyke the coast bends into Port Laing sands, and then takes a turn outwards till it passes Caroline's Nose, and then bends into the Ferry. Port Laing sands was our favourite resort. There we would amuse ourselves in many ways, and among others by picking up oyster shells and skimming them along the surface of the sea. Sometimes we would climb the face of the ground to the level of the plateau on which the cattle were grazing, and, if they were at some distance from us, make for the old farm-house; or take the narrow path along the steep coast line past Caroline's Nose till we came to the Ferry. Attractive as Port Laing was considered, I do not remember ever having seen any one there but ourselves and those with us ; and I was very often there. I certainly never saw any one bathing at the place. The Ferry does not seem to have been much resorted to at the time alluded to, as a summer residence ; or it had its own facilities for sea-bathing without resorting to Port Laing sands. The distance between the two was not great, although there was a little climbing to be done on both sides. It was at Port Laing I first learned that crabs (called "partans") hid themselves in the sand, for I dug them out of it, near the salmon stake-nets that were there.

Between the sand proper and the hill there was what geologists call a "raised beach," of a very little elevation, on which I have seen very fair crops reaped by old Adam ——, who made or used a very good road from the hill down to it. Between the cultivated ground and the sand there were some stones of considerable size and irregular shape, that could hardly be considered a fence made by the hand of man, although they served that purpose, but as if they had almost been left there by nature. Immediately near these stones, on the side facing the sea, yet not washed by it, there were some pretty specimens of what are to be found in such a place, that is, tall and stout stalks, with few leaves, bearing flowers of a delicate pink-like colour.

This sandy beach is associated in my memory with an adventure with two boys, a very little older than myself, getting a boat at Inverkeithing and leaving the bay in it. My first care was to lie down in the boat till it passed our pier, when we pulled along the shore in the direction of Port Laing, and out of what current there might have been. It was a small boat and easily managed, one oar being on one side near the bow, and two on the other side nearer the stern. We were wretched rowers, taking "spoonful about" with our oars. The other boys insisted on passing the sands, but I got frightened at the idea of going beyond the first head-land into a sea unknown to me, and refused to pull another stroke, when we returned, and got home in safety.

I have alluded to a loch on the top of the Ferry Hills, immediately back of Port Laing sands (p. 27). It was of a very small size, yet it had an artificial island in the middle of it, and a boat in the shape of a Norwegian skiff. I remember these two things particularly, because one day I saw a very attractive walking-stick on the island, when I immediately made for the boat, but found it padlocked, so that I had to take leave of the stick, on account of not being able to swim. Indeed I do not remember having even bathed in the sea; the aversion to which having apparently had its origin in the rough handling of our maid when she bathed me. But it was quite common for my father, when the tide suited, to leave the house in the morning, with nothing on him but a cloak and slippers, and avail himself of the excellent facilities that we had for sea-bathing.*

The loch spoken of had evidently been made or put in order by Mr. Cathcart, already alluded to, whose property, towards the west, and under the hill, adjoined it, with the high-road between them. In that case he must have got the consent of the owner and occupier of the land. The loch was kept in a very neat condition, and had the appearance of having been recently put in order, for the bank on the north side looked as if covered with a peat-like soil that had been thrown up from the bottom of it. The south side of this small sheet of water seemed flat and marshy. There were no trees or anything of that nature surrounding it.

Immediately below this loch, but a little to the right, is St. Margaret's

---

* Our usual bathing place was immediately behind the Lazaretto wall, where the rocks had been removed for the purpose. The people of the town who could swim bathed at the East Ness, and the others on the beach near the foundery. The water of the bay was pretty pure, judging from the fact that salt was made from it.

bay. This also was one of our favourite places of amusement, particularly when the wind was from the east. Saturday being house-cleaning day, all the children, after a hastily-got-up dinner, were, I might say, almost "turned out of doors" if the weather was suitable. Inside of the Lazaretto wall was frequently resorted to by us on such occasions when the weather or condition of the ground was questionable; but the hill looking down on St. Margaret's bay was frequently our choice. From the ground surrounding it we had a fine view of the five or six quarantine hulks at anchor in St. Margaret's Hope, and the ruins of Rosyth Castle, to the right, before alluded to (p. 27). The only dwelling in sight was the tollhouse. There is nothing particular to be said about this little bay, although it is not devoid of interest. The origin of its name has at least created a sentimental feeling in regard to it. I have a number of personal reminiscences connected with the place. First, there was a quarry of free or sand-stone immediately adjoining Mr. Cathcart's property of St. Margaret's, if it did not form part of it. It seems to have been opened to build his house; and never to have been resorted to for any other purpose. Its size indicated that. I frequently resorted to it with the blacksmith's dog for the purpose of swimming it in it, as it was easily reached by passing from his house behind the chemical works. To a child there is a peculiar awe-inspiring fascination connected with quarries and lochs of unknown depth. The stone of this quarry was evidently of superior quality, judging from my impression of it when compared with such in other places afterwards. And this estimation was confirmed by the fact that the stone used in the building of Beiner beacon towards the west, in 1841, by a Leith contractor, was taken from this quarry. On this occasion he must have dug a water-way to ship the stone from it; which seems to have led Captain Elder to convert it into a dock for his yacht. In my time there was no such water-way, although the tide when at its height merely entered it by a less than rill-like channel, which seems to have been made to get rid of the water gathering in it. It must have made an admirable dock of the kind, as it is almost completely surrounded by high lands; and it doubtless presents an interesting sight to a stranger when he views the yacht so securely protected in so unexpected a place.

Frequently I would go on Saturday afternoons to the neighbourhood of St. Margaret's bay with the Cruicks' ploughman. Once I recollect being with him, a little towards Rosyth, when he stopped his cart and pointed out the spot where, on passing long before daybreak for Charlestown for a load of lime, he was attacked by a bulldog coming out of a tinker's tent, when he took his "gully" and cut its throat. He displayed such feeling in his narrative as to leave in my mind no doubt of the truth of his assertion, which I listened to with awe.

On another occasion we went there, with Bob and Jess, tandem fashion, for a load of sea-sand. On arriving on the beach, the ploughman abruptly exclaimed, "Dear me, see how they fought till they killed each other," pointing to two dead yellow-hammers. "No," said I, with my familiarity with "scuffling," "that was not a fight; for had it been a fight the sand would have been disturbed, and the birds 'tousled.'" Some time before this it was asserted by the boys at the school that no one had ever found a dead sparrow. As these birds were very numerous about our place, as I have already said (p. 40), I thought I could find one, and sought diligently for it, without success. And so the finding of the two dead yellow-hammers attracted my special attention in regard to their condition and surroundings; but I could form no opinion on what was always a mystery to me. The birds lay very close together on sand that had not been disturbed by the elements since a high tide had passed over it some days before; in which condition the sand on the seashore always presents an attractive appearance. Nor did a feather of the birds present a ruffled or soiled appearance. How then did these two *cock* yellow-hammers get there? Such birds do not frequent the beach, away from where they nest, and particularly for the purpose of settling disputes. If they had been washed ashore by the tide, by what coincidence had they found their way into the sea, and been landed on the beach, almost touching each other, head to head?*

On another occasion when at the tollhouse at St. Margaret's bay, late in the evening, I got on the back of a gentleman's carriage going to the Ferry, and left it just before it entered the village, without being annoyed by any envious boy crying, "whip behind," for we did not even see a living creature of any kind on the way. I immediately started across the hills for home, and, as was my invariable custom, looked over the dyke to take a view of Port Laing sands, when I noticed, in the dusk of the evening, the only rabbit I ever saw on the peninsula. There were rabbit holes, and the usual indications of rabbits, but to me it was a surprise that I never met with one, although I always kept a sharp lookout for it. There was no place that would apparently suit for a rabbit-warren, so that the rabbits seemed to have got scattered, and to have kept under ground during the day. Under any circumstances they could not be numerous, and more especially as weasels were plentiful, and would keep down the rabbits, as they did

the rats about our place. The ground was common to almost any one, and there was not even the appearance of game-preserving; notwithstanding which hares were often met with, while formerly, by my father's account, they were numerous; and I recollect him pointing out the spot where he had "got one with each barrel." Sometimes, but not very often, a covey of partridges would be raised.

Adders (pronounced "ethers") or vipers were frequently met with near our place, where, as I have said before (p. 9), they had been numerous. With this animal I was familiar from my earliest recollection; and the allusion to it, or to any of the serpent tribe, at once attracts my attention. The last one I recollect seeing was immediately behind our house. It was lying upon the bare earth that connected the lower with the higher level of an abrupt breaking of the ground, and that had become warm by the rays of the sun. I was on my way to join my sisters near Port Laing sands, but I instantly stopped and made a detour to reach the place where they were. It was not a single viper I was afraid of, but of others that might be there.*

---

* I have written considerably on the subject of vipers (and certain other snakes) "swallowing their young," which has been denied by some people interesting themselves in natural history, although it is as much a fact as anything can be. This may be said to be the most interesting trait in the snake family, which should not be allowed to remain an open question. A further importance attaches to it as illustrative of the laws of evidence, that is, whether it or any other question should be decided according to evidence, or by the preconceived ideas of the world. The popular belief is in the affirmative, which makes it interesting to know how it originated. Then we have the evidence of people who have seen old snakes open their mouths and give refuge to their progeny, and taken them out of them. This they have done with *oviparous* snakes, whose eggs *are hatched in the soil*. *Viviparous*

---

* The yellow-hammer in Scotland generally is called the yorling, but in some places, as in Inverkeithing, the "yite." The male is a "little prince" of a bird.

The birds about our house were principally house and hedge or field sparrows, robins and wrens, blackbirds and thrushes, chaffinches and green linnets. All these were numerous. At a greater or less distance from the house they were, for the most part, and in considerable numbers, gray and rose linnets, yellow-hammers, and a bird called a "chir-maffit," that is, a mean-looking little bird, of a light brown colour, that generally built its nest, of long dry grass, among scraggy bramble bushes, near the road-side. When approached, its cry of "chir-rit" would be heard sometimes on this side of the road, and sometimes on that, without it making itself visible; which was so provoking that it would be stoned, and sometimes have its nest destroyed.

Skylarks and titlarks (called "titlies") were numerous. There was a considerable resemblance between the colours of their eggs, but those of the former were much the largest, while its nest was in its construction very inferior to that of the other. Titlarks would build their nests on the sides of ditches having a grass facing, or at the roots of whin sprouts, or such places. Skylarks were rather promiscuous in that respect. When the nest was in the midst of anything growing over or around it, the bird always alighted a little from it, and

by use made a well-beaten track to it. The birds were very little disturbed; so much so that the two kinds of larks would sometimes build their nests very close to the footpath, that would generally be passed by us once a day in both directions.—There was another bird, of a much shyer nature than the larks, that built its nest on the ground. It was apparently a little larger than a house sparrow, and its plumage was about equally divided into, I think, red, white and black. It was called a "coal-head." I never found more than three nests of this species; two with young ones, and one with eggs.

Sometimes the blackbird would build in singular places, even inside of the Lazaretto. I recollect, on entering it, being startled by the peculiar cry of this bird when forced to leave its nest. Looking up to a beam under the second floor, I saw the nest, and a row of others in every stage of ruins till the last one appeared to be a little rubbish. The bird, in short, had built a nest every season, adding it to the row of the preceding ones. Pieces of newspapers were often used by this bird when it built on a tree.

The robin was also sometimes capricious as to the place in which it would build its nest, although it was never far from a dwelling. It was generally on the rising side of a path

snakes are born either as the eggs are being dropped on the ground, or by their wriggling out of them after touching it ; which makes it impossible that the young of the viper, contained in eggs about the size of those of a blackbird, and measuring at birth about four and a half or five inches, could have been taken out of a mother, by White of Selborne, *free of the eggs*, and upwards of seven inches in length, unless they had entered her by the mouth. Objections have been advanced that the phenomenon is impossible, for the reason that there is no room in the *stomach* and *among the vital organs* for the young ones ; while the fact is that they do not enter that part of the mother, but take refuge in the chamber that contained them when in the eggs.

The evidence on this question I submitted last December to the publishers of the *Encyclopædia Britannica*, with the idea that justice will be done to it in the article on the *Reptilia* when it appears. In the last edition the subject was not noticed, either because it was accidentally or purposely omitted, or was doubted or denied, or because the writer or editor would not assume the responsibility of maintaining the affirmative, in the face of what he might look upon as the ridicule of a certain part of society. In the forthcoming article on the *Reptilia*, the question, it is hoped, will be settled "once for all," so that it may never again come up for discussion. If it is again omitted, the article will have left out what might be said to be "the most interesting trait in the snake family."

that was seldom used, or near the top of ground that presented a broken edge, or under a small isolated bush; but never in or on anything that could be moved, or in a field as such. One nest I found in long grass near a brier, very close to the sea, on ground that rose a little; and another near the top of what had the appearance of an attempt at the making of an open well of little depth. On the other hand I knew of one inside of our disused byre. The birds entered by a hole in the door, and built in the furthest and highest part, where I had to lift a tile to see the progeny. The only time I disturbed a robin was under the following circumstances. I was nesting behind the second house west of ours (the one that had been occupied by Mark Hadden and Giles), as I was on my way to school, when a robin suddenly flew out of the brae-side, so near me as almost to touch me. I had some trouble in finding the nest, which was reached by a hole, little larger than would admit the bird, through a long and thick fringe of wire-like grass that hung over an abrupt breaking of the ground. I thought over the subject when at the school, and, notwithstanding the popular feeling in regard to the bird, resolved to catch it on my way home; which I attempted by clapping my cap on the hole, when the robin instantly glided past me. "Two holes," said I in my chagrin, and, on examining the place closely, I noticed an open space between the grassy fringe and the ground it overlapped. On finding that the bird had abandoned its eggs, I regretted what I had done; although the fact of there being two holes made as lasting an impression on me as if they had been purposely prepared for safety.*

The crested plover or lapwing or "pee-weep" did not build on the peninsula, although it would occasionally be seen on it singly or in pairs. I knew of only one wood pigeon's nest, on the small young plantation back of Port Laing sands, alluded to (pp. 27 and 35). I have said that this piece of wood was "of about an acre." It might not have exceeded half an acre. It certainly was nearly square, and had apparently been well laid out, but had been neglected, for whins had been allowed to grow to a good height inside of it.

Having so many house-sparrows about our place, we had frequent visits from sparrow-hawks, which sometimes showed a wonderful temerity, as the following instance will illustrate. One evening, when it was nearly dusk, I noticed, from a window in our sitting-room, one of these birds eating something, at a very short distance from the house, and I directed my father's attention to it. It was late for almost any kind of bird to be abroad, and especially to be feeding; but late as it was it could be seen that it was a sparrow-hawk. My father then told me to sit still, while he opened the door in sight of the bird, which faced us, and going behind the house passed round by the Lazaretto wall to take it in the rear. I waited patiently till he made his appearance, hat in hand, and got very near the hawk, when it flew away. I immediately left the house to see what it had been eating, when I found that it had carried off its prey, leaving only a few fea-

---

* The house mentioned, I omitted to say, on a former occasion, was the property of two maiden sisters, probably past middle life, who owned the land on part of which the Lazaretto was built, as I always understood. One summer, for the purpose of sea-bathing, they used the upper floor, which was entered by a stair behind, at a right angle with the building. At all other times it was unoccupied. These ladies were tall and plain in their appearance, and unpretentious in their dress and habits. They were very quiet and kindly, but not inclined to be social. I never was inside of the part of the house occupied by them; and I felt disappointed at never having had my curiosity gratified by a sight of it.

thers behind. I could not but smile at the idea of a person trying to "catch a hawk" by getting in the ·rear of it and dropping his hat over it.

When I lived at the Lazaretto I enjoyed to the full the charms of bird-nesting. But rearing of birds in the house was discouraged, while blowing and stringing their eggs was prohibited. Occasionally I would join other boys at "blind smashie," that is, an egg would be placed on the ground and we would shut our eyes and advance on it. But I never did that of my own accord. However, I remember taking a bird that was pretty well fledged and putting it on a nest of eggs on which another had been incubating, and at a short distance watching the result of the intending mother finding another sitting on *her* eggs, when I was glad to put the young bird where I had found it.

Being often in the quarantine watch-house, I had many stories told me by the old boatmen of mermaids combing their hair on the rocks at low water. I really believed what these old men told me, and pictured to myself these apocryphal animals on the island of Inchcolm; the sound of the word contributing to the illusion of them "*combing*" their hair" on it. Now and then a seal would pop its head above water, which I at first imagined might be one of the mermaids. Speaking of Inchcolm, I might say that the island and the ruins on it were associated in my mind with feelings which it would be difficult to describe.

The natural products of the Cruicks' peninsula, especially in the neighbourhood and back of our place, might be said to be whin and bramble bushes and ferns; and if cultivation had been discontinued the ground would soon have become covered with them. Not even a sprig of heather did I ever find there. The wild flowers that attracted us the most were bluebells and primroses; and it was our invariable custom to search for the first appearance of the latter, so that we came to know where to go for them. Bramble bushes were very common between our house and Port Laing sands; and from Henderson's dyke to that sandy beach the rocks on the seashore were fringed with what might be called a magnificent growth of them. The fruit of these we would occasionally use, particularly at the opening of the season, and on Saturday afternoons, when we would "take to the hills" during house-cleaning. On such occasions the oldest girl, who was in every way of a superior character, and much looked up to by the others, generally took the lead; and a taste which she had for what might be called botany added to the feeling of deference which we all showed her. The second girl claimed the exclusive right to take charge of the youngest child, and lead or carry it, as might be; and her peaceable, disinterested and obliging disposition would have been sorely tried, if any of the others had attempted to dispute her claim. The third girl and I did all the quarreling there was, and it was frequent and sometimes bitter. She would catch at my phrases and actions and turn them into ridicule. She would say, "Watch him, just watch him, and you will see him show his airs!" This she would do even before company, where she would keep her eye fixed on me, and if I even moved she would point her finger at me and loudly exclaim, "There, he shows his airs!" This was very provoking, and would have justified a thrashing, if I had resorted to that for redress.

During my recollection, which extends over 1831-5, I do not remember any violent winds. Our house was well protected from the effects of such by the quarantine premises on the east, and pretty well by the ground in the other directions, saying nothing of the trees surrounding it; so that, at night especially, we were sometimes hardly aware of the wind being high. Had there been violent storms from the east, the effects of them must have been more or less seen on the coast back of our place towards the Ferry; but I never saw such. The same can be said of snow storms. I do not remember ever having been kept from going to school on account of them. We had always a method of escaping the effects of snow in that respect, for the tide swept the edge of the bay of it, so that we could easily go along it; which, however, proved destructive to shoes, in consequence of the effects of salt water on them. The state of the tide was a matter of constant thought; not that it ever prevented us going to and returning from the town, but merely influenced us in the way by which we would do it. Personally it was attractive to me, both when I got up in the morning, and when I left the school for home. And as early impressions are the most lasting, the sea in its ebb and flow has always been a subject of special interest to me.

It would be incorrect for me to say that I could still go over the Cruicks' peninsula blindfolded, although I think that, in that condition, I could describe pretty correctly to one with me, the directions and turns of the roads and paths, the configuration of the ground, the knolls and what grew on them, the few trees, and the simple objects on it, when I lived there. Even the state of the weather and atmosphere on certain occasions, and especially the snow scenes, could be recalled by me. There is hardly a spot on it that would not elicit, not one but frequently several reminiscences connected with it. My favourite place was the highest ridge between Port Laing sands and St. Margaret's bay, where I often sat with the Cruicks' herd-boy, who was three or four years older than myself.

It was near this spot that I discovered that there was such a place as the North Queensferry, although it was only about a mile from our place. I often heard people speaking of "the ferry," which I understood to be the one on the south side of the firth.

Some time after I began to go to the school at Inverkeithing I happened to say to the herd that a Ferry boy attending it had a long way to go home, pointing to the west, as if he had to travel around the water to reach it; so crude were my ideas in that respect. The herd, with the greatest astonishment, said, "There's the Ferry," pointing in the direction of it, when I made for the brow of the hill and surveyed it with all the feelings attending a discovery.

While on the top of the ridge mentioned, a gale suddenly sprung up from the west, when the herd said, "Now we will see it strike the sea on the other side," where it was perfectly smooth. Very soon the water became ruffled as the wind reached it over the hill, at quite a distance from the shore; towards which it remained calm, and would have given ample protection to a vessel seeking shelter near it.

On another occasion we picked up a dog that had lost its master. It presented a forlorn appearance when met with, but soon it seemed to feel at home in our company. Its eyes were of different colours. "That one," said the herd, "is for sheep, and this one for cattle"; which had some truth in it, as I found on meeting the dog the same year in Leith, when I asked its master if he had not lost it lately. Yes, he said, he had lost it on the Ferry Hills. It turned out that it was good for both sheep and cattle.

At another time the herd said to me, "Come and I will show you something"; and, going towards the dyke at the road, he lifted a piece of sod, and putting his hand into a hole, brought out a young rabbit. He had come across a nest of them, and, judging of the direction of it, cut out the sod and dug down to the nest, and replaced the sod till the rabbits were old enough to be taken. This was the only nest of rabbits I knew of on the peninsula, although I had heard of other boys occasionally finding them. The sight of the young rabbits interested me greatly; nor could I help observing how cunningly the old rabbit had closed the mouth of the hole by throwing back the earth on it, and what skill or experience it required to find a rabbit's nest.

One day he showed me a pretty large stone supported by many small sticks, and asked me if I knew how he had succeeded in doing it. On confessing my ignorance he knocked it over, and propped it up with small stones, which he removed as he inserted the sticks in their place, till the large stone appeared as when first shown to me.

Some time after this there were opposition steamers—I think the *Stirling Castle* and the *Dumbarton Castle*—running between Leith (Newhaven) and Stirling, both starting at the same time from Newhaven, pretty well on in the evening. It was always interesting to us to see them approach and pass the Ferry, particularly as each of us had his favourite boat, and wished it success. This was the first racing between steamers that I saw.

A brother of this boy, when at the place mentioned, one day wished to get some milk from one of the cows, to mix with peasemeal to feed a nest of drooping birds that he carried about with him, in a small, round receptacle made of twisted straw, and having a lid. Both of us knew that this was an unpardonable offense; still, with the dread of Nell, at the farm-house, before us, we managed to catch and hold the cow for the purpose wanted.

One day on going home from school along the beach I noticed that it was strewn with "garvies," which had been washed ashore; and that each wave landed some still in life. With the latter I filled my pocket-handkerchief, with a view to treating our cat, if no other use would be made of them. On passing the ruinous houses near the edge of the bay, so frequently alluded to, I stopped to have some gossip with the herd-boy, and put my bundle of fish on the ground, and moved further up the hill with him. On leaving for home I found that one of the cows had just finished swallowing both fish and handkerchief. It was then I first learned that cows will eat fish, partly, I dare say, for the salt contained in them, of which they are fond; and yet I do not remember ever having seen the cows "salted" at the farm-house. It seems that that is never or hardly ever done in Scotland, although I found pieces of rock-salt in fields in which sheep were kept; placed there apparently for their use.

I have said (p. 7) that the Cruicks' farm-house "stood about a third of a mile from the Lazaretto." It might have been half a mile. I was often there, and I have a very fair recollection of how the farm was managed, and what kinds of work were done when the weather would not admit of anything being attended to out-of-doors, and particularly in regard to making straw-rope for thatching the following season. Messages between our house and that of the farm were generally carried by me; but anything of weight was borne by the maid. One morning, either because she had got up late or was very busy with her work, I was asked to go for the family's milk, with a tin pitcher of a size that could almost hold what would fill a small pail. I took the path straight for the farm, which crossed a ploughed field, between it and our house; over which, to the extent of about a fourth of the whole distance, we always exercised the right of way, whatever might have been sown or planted on it. I noticed that the ground was so wet and slippery that I could not safely return by it with my burden. On leaving the farm-house with the milk, Nell expressed a doubt whether I could carry it home, when I said that I thought I could do it; and she stood at the door looking at me for a short time after I left it. In place of going straight to our house by the way I came, I turned to the left, and walked on the grass as far as Pinkie well, near the beach, from which a path led to our house; thus forming two sides of a triangle, and making the distance to be travelled considerably greater than by the way I set out. What with the weight carried, and not being accustomed to such work, I felt completely "done up"; and so I put the pitcher on a grassy spot, nearly surrounded by whin bushes, and started for home, after seeing that neither "beast nor body" was within sight, and casting a look behind to see that it remained as I had placed it. The maid was sent to bring it home, and I was told that she found it safe, but the milk spilt. Whether that was true or not, I was rewarded for my pains by being dubbed "Coup the milk" for many days. For the future my only thought in regard to the milk was to see that I got my share of it, however it was brought into the house.

I have frequently alluded to the herds, some of whom were really decent lads, but occasionally there would be, in every sense of the word, a "blackguard boy" among them. Indeed many distinguished Scotchmen have herded cows in their youth. The very word "herd-boy," as applicable to Scotland, stirs in my breast a feeling of sympathy, as I know well what it means, having come next to being one myself. Generally I had no others outside of our family even to speak to near home. Their employment was a monotonous one; and glad were they to meet one besides the dumb creatures they attended to. The feelings of association were mutual. My father's official, personal, and social stand-ing in such a small community always secured for me the boys' respectful regard in every way; and in return I treated them with kindness. However quarrelsome I might have been with others, I never had the heart to be so with the herd-boys; but I would be of service to them in many ways. If they built their fires near our house, I would find them lights and coal. In that respect I was once rather too kind to them, for I appropriated to their (and my own) use a piece of peat that served the purpose of cleaning the irons for dressing clothes. This had become hard and glazed by age and use; and although it was missed, suspicion did not fall on me, and as nothing was said to me about it, I also kept silent on the subject.

Saturday afternoons were the usual times when we would have our fires, which were generally at a braeside, or in some way more or less sheltered, yet so that the herd-boy could keep his eye on his charge when he happened to be with us. We would on such occasions roast shell-fish—crabs, limpets, and whelks —and potatoes and mushrooms, according to the season, dispensing with tea and supper in consequence; and we would linger over the fires till it would get so late that the maid would be sent in search of us.

Speaking of fires in the fields reminds me of getting a light before lucifer matches were invented or had come into use. The invariable custom was to prepare the kitchen fire for the morning by letting it get pretty well down before retiring for the night, and placing on it a thick piece of coal nearly of the size of the grate, and drawing the cinders and ashes around the edges of it. In the morning the coal would generally be about two-thirds burned, and the rest of it so dry and inflammable that on being broken up in the morning a good fire could be easily made. If the "gathering coal" happened to go out, a light would be got by going to a neighbour with a lantern ready for use. A very important thing in using coal was to lay aside such pieces of it as would suit for "gathering" or "resting" purposes.

But the primitive mode of getting a light was by using flint and steel and tinder, and "spunks," that is, as I have already said, "splints of wood dipped in brimstone." I do not remember having noticed this apparatus in our house; I certainly never saw it used there. But I often witnessed the getting of a light in this way by the boatmen in the quarantine watch-house. They would produce a small tin box with a lid, inside of which were some burned or charred rags, which would catch the spark coming from the flint and steel. This would be gently blown upon after a little of the tinder had been drawn together by the "spunk," the sulphur at the end of which would produce the light wanted. Getting a light in this way was an easy matter after daybreak; but it must have been different in the dark, although necessity and use lessened what would be found on trial to be a trouble nowadays. Getting a light out-of-doors was by flint and steel or the back of a pocket-knife blade and a piece of match, that is, loose-made paper that had been steeped in saltpetre, or rubbed by bruised and moistened gunpowder. This mode doubtless is still occasionally used by old people when lighting their pipes.

In the watch-house, as I might have said on a former occasion, there were two boatmen who lived, that is, cooked and slept there after the cholera in 1832, and left it some time in 1833. One of them, who was much younger than the other, did not present a single salient point (excepting his large size) by which I could remember him; even his name I do not recollect, if I ever heard it. The other one was a gray-haired man who was generally spoken of as "Old John Hamilton," and was pretty-well liked. He was always neatly-dressed in blue cloth, and was very tidy in his person. This might have been his Sunday "rig," for all the work he had to do. With much of the "sea-dog" in his countenance, he was considerably shrunken in the lower part of his body. He had arrived at that age when a discharge on a pension was soon to be expected. Latterly these two men had nothing to do but "kill" their time in the best way they could. Most of it was spent in pacing to and fro, sometimes on one side of the Lazaretto wall and sometimes on the other; and, when the weather was cold, in slapping their hands under their arm-pits, to keep their blood in circulation when in the open air. Sometimes they would gossip on the pier with Andrew Stewart, the pilot, as he made his appearance with his Norwegian skiff and spy-glass. So far as I noticed they were not readers. The uncertainty of the continuance of the quarantine establishment doubtless fretted them; and old John, who had naturally a voice that both creaked and croaked, showed it peculiarly in his querulous impatience about his official disposal. "Any news from Borrowstounness?" (the local official headquarters) was his constant question; and he harped so much on this one string, that even a child got tired of hearing the word mentioned.[*] John's age, face, and voice and slightly boisterous way evidently made him "captain of the watch," and left the other little to say on almost any occasion.

According to McCulloch's *Commercial Dictionary* (1869), there are, at least were, eight places in England for vessels performing quarantine; and two in Scotland—Inverkeithing Bay for the east coast of Scotland, and Holy Loch in the Firth of Clyde, for the west coast. The vessels destined for the Inverkeithing Station during the cholera of 1832 either

---

[*] John's pronunciation of the word was Borstonness, which was the current one in the place. Nowadays it is Bo'ness.

proceeded direct to St. Margaret's Hope after being boarded at Leith, or first hove to a little to the south and east of the Lazaretto before going there. I recollect my father saying that on a foreign vessel not "heaving to" he ordered one of the boatmen to raise a musket, when those on board instantly dipped below the bulwarks, but soon peered over the edge of them, and again disappeared at the sight of it, till they came to understand what was wanted. This musket was doubtless unloaded and carried under the regulations adopted before or during the long wars, so recently ended, and still continued in force.

The only occasion I remember of a vessel "riding quarantine" at St. Margaret's Hope after 1832 was one bound for Leith from Alexandria, about 1842. Her English owners, in anticipation of her arrival, at first wished her to conform with the regulations at Standgate Creek, in or near the Thames, not knowing that St. Margaret's Hope, about twelve miles distant, was so convenient for the vessel. She had on board some flax, which was one of the enumerated articles "considered as most liable to infection"; and even then I think she was detained only about fourteen days, while the term "quarantine" implies forty days or six weeks. From the fact of the Lazaretto at Inverkeithing having been abolished, it is presumed that the same took place at the other Stations; and that quarantine is now occasionally performed by vessels remaining a certain time, according to circumstances, separated from the community, like the one referred to at St. Margaret's Hope.

For some time previous to the cholera of 1832, the services of my father at the Lazaretto could not have been much more than nominal; and it is difficult to imagine how he and the boatmen could have managed to pass their time. I knew, as a matter of tradition, that, while the public service was doubtless well attended to, there had been frequent excursions in the neighbourhood; which the boatmen were apt to enjoy, especially when eating and drinking made part of them. I remember the appearance of the boat used on such occasions. It was large in size, full in the beam, not high above the water-line, very conveniently seated towards the stern, and of a handsome model, but apparently not heavy enough for man-of-war purposes; the very ideal of a boat for pleasure excursions. The annual expense connected with the establishment, including the feu duty or ground rent, did not probably exceed £400, while the original cost of the buildings might not have exceeded £1,200, or £1,500 at the most; not a heavy burden for the whole of the east coast of Scotland.

My acquaintance with the "wide world" at this time extended no further than strolling over the Cruicks' Peninsula, and going to and returning from school, with the following exceptions, not including three trips to Rosyth Castle, and visiting Limekilns, as mentioned.

One day I arranged for an expedition to Fordel with the two boys in whose company I found my way into the school porch (p. 37), to get bark to make bird-lime, which I think was the only really lawless adventure I engaged in. At this time Fordel was in the possession of Admiral Sir Philip Durham; three of the children of whose factor attended the school I did. St. Davids was the shipping port for the coal mined on the estate, if it did not belong to it. The harbour was small, but convenient in every way, and well protected from every wind, and of easy access. I believe it admitted vessels of 600 tons; the tide receding a very little way from the end of the pier, if it even did that. There was a house with a circular-like front, painted white, facing the Lazaretto, and in which there was a clear light at night, which attracted our special notice. To the left were some salt-pans that sent up a heavy volume of smoke. Above these, and nestling under the eastern side of Letham wooded hill, was a farm-house occupied by a widow, three of whose children attended the school I went to. But I never had my curiosity gratified in regard to the appearance of the ground behind St. Davids.

I have said (p. 27) that "Scotch boys then were not partial to visiting places that were strange to them, unless when with others that were familiar with them," as "they became suspicious of everybody and everything, when strolling out of what might be called their districts." The two boys mentioned lived a little in the direction of Fordel, and were pretty-well known there. We first visited the factor's house, which seemed an awkward-looking building, facing an open space, with its back towards Inverkeithing. After going there as friends, we proceeded on our return to get the bark in the "policy" on the western side of a pretty-wide road that led in the direction of St. Davids. I was not aware of the kind of bark that was wanted, and when I found that it was of the holly, I hesitated in touching it from my regard to it, as we had only one of' the kind at our place; and it was much prized for its brilliant green leaves, which were strong and armed all round with hard and sharp spikes,—a protection in itself, and a notice to people not to touch it. Then there were its beautiful red berries during the winter. When everything else was bare, this evergreen presented a lovely appearance, and especially in the snow. While nature seemed dead, the holly appeared alive, and, excepting the ivy, was the only evergreen we had. I was still more attached to this tree (if tree it could be called), which was inside of the Lazaretto wall, from having found almost immediate-

ly under it a robin's nest, which I watched from the time it contained eggs till the young took flight. If I had had any idea that by stripping the stem of the holly of its bark, the tree would be destroyed, I would doubtless not have touched it. As it was, I got the two boys to act as sentinels while I cut the bark from the tree, and divided the spoil. I was told that the bird-lime was made by boiling and beating the bark; and so I attempted the operation, which came to nothing, as I was not allowed the use of a pot at home, and had the bark thrown out-of-doors.

When at school the boys mentioned kept showing me walnuts, and their hands stained with the husks of them, without taking me into their confidence as to where they had got them; which was a breach of what was an understanding between us, that we were to share in everything. It was some time before I learned that the nuts were got from trees at Balbougie farm-house; but when I went there with another boy in search of them I was too late, for not one was to be seen on the trees or on the ground. As it was, this small walnut grove proved to me the "end of the earth" in that direction. The name of this fine farm always sounded pleasantly to me. It was tenanted by a short and thick-set oldish man, who had two boys at our school, and who always occupied the "seat of honour" at the examination of it.

Scott's Mill was reached by going from the Boreland farm along the "cast," that is, water led from the dam there to the distillery. I was only twice at this mill, the first time being to buy rabbits. It was driven by water that came from the direction of Fordel. When I heard of Hercules cleaning a stable by turning a river into it, I thought that that was no great "labour," for it would have been an easy matter to have turned the "cast" into Inverkeithing mill-dam, and "mucked the byre" attached to the bridge there, in which were kept oxen belonging to the distillery. At Scott's Mill there lived a boy who was lost in the steamship *President* on her return voyage from New York, while acting as second or third engineer, in the early part of 1841. I have a very distinct recollection of him in 1835, and can almost recall the sound of his voice. He sat on one of the most advanced forms (holding two scholars each), facing the two end windows, his being next the church. He was a good-looking boy, neatly dressed in light-coloured moleskin ; was a good scholar, fairly peaceable, and well-behaved ; and was of a superior character, but with a good share of confidence in himself, and faultfinding in others. I recollect how sadly I felt on hearing of his early and pitiful end. The little mill mentioned, situated as it were in the vale, presented a sleepy-looking object in the landscape. Its dam was a subject of interest to me, owing to its being frequented by " water hens," which stirred my curiosity to see in what respect they differed from ordinary hens ; but I never had it gratified, nor the opportunity of tracing the water towards its source.

The little village called Hillend, near the upper end of Letham Hill (which is said to be now entirely occupied by Irish), is associated in my memory mainly with its teacher, of the name of Scotland, having been thrashed by his scholars ; and by the second boy of the family asking "if it was Scotland o' Hillend that was told to draw the sword," on hearing our maid singing, " Draw the sword, Scotland." It was also the headquarters of a rather peculiar man who " whipped the cat " around the country, that is, tailored from house to house.

My last expedition was to Dunfermline, in the latter part of the summer of 1835, in company with my parents and two oldest sisters, while the youngest one was left at home. On our way to it my father on cutting a switch from a hedge was gruffly taken to task for it by a ploughman, who was immediately " placated " by him saying, " Come to my place and cut as many switches as you please." We passed through the arch at the Abbey on our way to " Inglis'," a famous dealer in all kinds of " soft goods," whose shop, on a pretty-wide street, looked towards the Forth, perhaps on a line leading to St. Margaret's Bay or Rosyth Castle. I was accustomed to the little cribs of shops at Inverkeithing ; but when I entered Inglis' large establishment, in which were a number of well-dressed men bare-headed, I instantly took off my cap, and was sharply told by my father to put it on ; so that I erred on the safe side on *that* occasion. Various purchases were made preparatory to our leaving for Leith, among which was a pair of braces for my father, which I remember particularly, owing to having seen him a short time before repairing his old ones. Another purchase was blue cloth to make a suit for the third boy of the family, who had just recovered from an attack of typhus fever, as mentioned (p. 43). On my asking why the articles purchased were not bought in Inverkeithing, I was told that nothing but trash could be got there, and that " Inglis' " was the place to go to for such goods. The same might have been said of the local tailor, who was told to make the child's clothes " pretty big for a growing laddie " ; for we were all mortified, on arriving at Leith, at seeing good cloth converted into a wretched garment, when the very prepossessing child—with his blue eyes, curly fair hair, and rosy complexion—entitled him to at least what would have looked decent.

After doing our shopping we went to a place for refreshments, which did not consist of a great variety, as mutton pies were the only things to be had in the way of pastry. On our way home we were overtaken by the two doctors who had attended the child mentioned, riding in a gig, when a conversation ensued, during which I got close to the gig and applied my hand to the spokes of one of the wheels as it revolved. They seemed to think that I was fishing for a ride, for they stopped the gig and asked me to get into it, which I did with great celerity.* We soon left the pedestrians far behind. I got out at the foot of the hill that led to Inverkeithing, and made for home by crossing the high ground where there was a gap opposite the road along the beach that led to our house. Riding in a gig, and between two doctors at that, had such an effect upon me that I was in a humour to quarrel with anybody; but as I met no one on the way, I immediately sought out my youngest sister, with whom I had always an open or running account in that line. I have said that she would "catch at my phrases and actions and turn them into ridicule" (p. 61). Among the former I remember that I used to ask, not merely if a thing was for eating, or swallowing, but "is this for swallowing over your throat?" When she saw me eating anything outside of a meal she would say, "Oh, yes, that's for swallowing over your throat!" I found that during our absence at Dunfermline she had made jelly from brambles, and had it nicely set out in dishes in the open air, waiting the arrival of her two sisters. On this occasion I did not ask if what I saw was for "swallowing over your throat," but did it without ceremony, thus "showing my airs" in the most offensive manner. It would be hard to say which of us was most to blame in these squabbles. Even when she would voluntarily help me at my lessons at night, which she often did, especially when writing "meanings," that is, the definition of words, it would be "cat and dog" between us. At night she would also prettily sing duets with my oldest sister, which were greatly improved by attending a singing class, along with other three of the family, including myself, of whom nothing could be made, except that I would appreciate and enjoy the singing of others. The teacher was a "professor" from Dunfermline, of the name of R——, whose class was in the top story of the town-hall of Inverkeithing, on the floor of which he chalked his music, in place of on a board against the wall. One day we had him to dinner, when he brought my oldest sister's piano, and it was then I first had an opportunity of closely observing a "singing man." He gave us during the afternoon and evening both playing and singing in abundance, which I greatly admired, as well as the way in which he enjoyed his dinner and toddy. He was about or past middle life, medium in height, pursy in person, and a *bon-vivant* in his habits.

I recollect having been at one time in "perfect accord" with my youngest sister, but it did not last long. Of the Lazaretto I have said that "the last use I made of the place was to kill, for the table, the rabbits I had running at large" (p. 20). My father had fixed a day for doing that, but my youngest sister, the night before, suggested to me that we should get up early in the morning and do it. Her proposal astonished me, but I instantly entered into it with spirit. I do not recollect who awoke the other, but we got up

---

* One of these doctors, of the name of B——, had succeeded to the local practice of the one mentioned as having acted for the Government during the cholera, and who had recently left for America (pp. 36, 42, and 45); on which occasion there was a strong feeling shown by the inhabitants on losing him. The three members of our family mentioned (p. 43), were among the new doctor's first patients. The two girls he managed easily, but he had to call in a well-known Dunfermline doctor of the name of D——, (the other one in the gig), in the case of the boy, which was a very critical one. For a barber to shave his head they got the old Inverkeithing weaver whom I have alluded to on two occasions (pp. 17 and 49).

very early for the work. She armed herself with a long stick, with which she smote one of the rabbits over the back, when I said, " Hold on, that's not the way to kill a rabbit "; and seizing the disabled one by the hind legs, I gave it a sharp blow behind the ears with the outside edge of the hand. "That's the way to do it," I continued, and told her to help me to catch the others, which were disposed of in the same way. After getting through with our job, by which we earned our breakfasts, we looked at each other as if we had been criminals, and I agreed to say nothing of her in connection with it. With much misgiving on my part, I carried my load of dead rabbits to my father, without a remark of any kind, when he, with the greatest good-humour, merely asked me if I had got them all—apparently pleased that I had saved him trouble. When the rabbits were brought to the table, my assistant in the killing of them craned her neck to get a sight of them, and instantly left the room, for the reason that she was sick and could eat nothing ; so that to allay the alarm, I had to explain matters. I had no such squeamishness ; perhaps for the reason of the rabbits having been running at large, so different from what might have been the case, had they been kept in a hutch.

I have frequently alluded to Mr. Cathcart's house at St. Margaret's, which was built some time after 1829, about which year he occupied our house for sea-bathing, as mentioned (p. 6). There was this peculiarity about the house, that it could not be seen from the land, except from near Rosyth Castle. From it there was a fine view of both sides of the Forth to the west, the sunsets being peculiarly attractive.* At first it was

very much exposed from the lack of trees, which led a person, while on the steamboat on the way to Stirling, and in the hearing of Mr. Cathcart, to make a very disparaging remark in regard to its owner, but which I need not repeat. By having occupied our house, a close intimacy and friendship sprung up between him and my father, who was often at his house till the day we left the neighbourhood. Mr. Cathcart had indeed no great choice of neighbours, which seems to have led him to appreciate my father, who, without any apparent personal pretense of the nature to be offensive, or desire for society, was yet suitable for any company into which he might enter. It was always an interesting sight to see Mr. Cathcart and his young family walking to church (for they never drove to it). Frequently, as they left St. Margaret's bay, and we went along the beach of Inverkeithing bay, we would meet on our way to church ; or, the one company would walk slowly for the other to make up to it on the occasion. Mr. Cathcart was a very tall, handsome, fine-looking, and dignified man, who had a habit of lifting his hat and wiping his forehead in warm weather. His wife, who was matronly in her figure, and of a fair height, looked short when walking alongside of him. The daughters, I think, were of a pretty-fair complexion, and seemed to "take after" their mother. The oldest son, who was tall of his age and fine-looking, wore a tall white beaver hat, and appeared of a different order from the boys of the neighbourhood. Brown seemed to be the favourite colour of the family in the matter of dress.

It must have been shortly after Mr. Cathcart's house was built that I

* I sometimes saw fine sunsets as well as moonlight scenes while looking west from near this place. The five or six large quarantine hulks had a very striking appearance on such occasions. In the graveyard of Limekilns there is said to be the tombstone of a sea-faring man, with an inscription beginning with the words, "At anchor now in death's dark road—" in evident allusion to St. Margaret's Hope in front of the place.

was first at it with my parents, possibly on some such occasion as "house-heating," for I remember but two circumstances connected with the visit, which might be called "salient points." I was naturally excited when going to a house of that kind, and felt astonished at seeing a horse inside of it, on the door being opened; for up to this time I had never seen anything in the imitation of a horse, except a small toy on wheels, or something in a shop window that could be eaten. This seemed to me a real horse in the lobby, which was very roomy, compared to the narrow passage into our little house, on the right hand side of which hung a heavy navy pistol and a marine's cartridge-box. When I saw how the horse "ran," I soon got on its back, and behaved very much like a certain personage when mounted on a real one. The other "salient point" was quite in keeping with this one, for, as I got through with my tea (it being an afternoon visit), I bawled out, "Mamma, I'm done," which caused an instant silence, and led all present to look in my direction, and the lady of the house to remark, "What does he say?" To this no reply was made, and the rudeness passed off. I was doubtless corrected afterwards. I certainly never repeated the words at home, and I have still a sensitive feeling of having committed myself and others on the occasion.

Speaking of horses reminds me of the first one I saw, which was an old white one that grazed around the Lazaretto with the farmer's cows. It was too old to do work of consequence or perhaps any kind of labour. It had a habit of scratching itself more than ordinary, and as there were no trees there it would throw itself on its back and turn over and over. One turn was the gain of a shoe ; a return made a pair. I frequently saw it earn a complete set without getting on its feet ; such was the feeling and almost the belief of the herd and myself, who would whistle to help the "poor beast" in its labours. Of asses, called "cuddies," I recollect having seen a kind of a fight between a grown-up boy and one of them, as to whether or not it should be allowed to bray, when the boy applied his hands to its mouth to prevent it. But the "cuddy" had the best of it, although its music was considerably marred by the attempt at stopping it.

Almost immediately adjoining St. Margaret's, in the direction of the Ferry, was the little one-storied farm-house called the Ferry Barns, situated on some low-lying ground near the sea, and not, I think, observable from the road above it, unless from the brow of the hill leading down to it. It was a primitive building, covered, if I mistake not, with thatch, and had a little garden on the west side of it, in which were some fine gooseberries, the most attractive things there to me. I was often there. This little farm-house (if such it could be called), and that of the Cruicks, were the only ones in use on the peninsula. From the Ferry Barns to the school-house (in which the tenant, a very little man, had been teacher), on the north side of the road, extended the planted ground of Captain Macconnochie, on whose property I never was.

The Ferry itself I have already alluded to (pp. 55 and 62). It was long after I became aware of the existence of the place that I ventured into it ; but I would frequently go as far as the brow of the hill, where the school-house was, and look at it from that spot. The reason for this was the aversion which, as I have said, Scotch boys had to stray into strange places Gradually I got into the habit of sometimes strolling there by going errands for the family ; on which occasions I held that I had a right to be there, and feeling very brave would say to myself, "Wha daur meddle wi' me ?" One day after I had got accustomed to visit the village the captain of the old rickety steam ferry-boat told me to "jump aboard," when I made a trip to the South Queens-ferry, which was an important event in my experience there.

The school at the Ferry seemed to meet the wants of the place, except that occasionally scholars from it would find their way to the school of Inverkeithing to "finish" their edu-cation. I recollect but six such—four boys and two girls. The last two boys were big fellows who always kept together, apparently for defence, for they were never seen in the town except when hurrying to and from school, as if they dreaded the enmity of all belonging to the place. They might have been described as "Cun-ning and Cruelty." On one occasion, when outside of the town, they seized a little boy, who had perhaps insulted them, and crammed his mouth with what they found on the highway. The feeling between the children of the two places, as was common in Scotland, could not be called friend-ly, although it never, in my experi-ence, led to actual hostilities. The behaviour of each set was regulated by their being in the camp of the other. Thus I remember, when at the Ferry with three Inverkeithing boys, that it was not the grown-up people nor the dogs that we were afraid of, but boys of our own age and those of a larger growth. My complete identity with Inverkeithing seems to have influenced me at first in my relation to the Ferry. The feeling alluded to was even manifest-ed, but in a less degree, towards the Ferry girls that attended our school. I recollect going home from it on a Saturday forenoon with the two men-tioned—one a big, coarse-looking girl, almost a woman, wearing a brown beaver bonnet and a fur tippet that had seen better days; and the other a blue-eyed, rosy-cheeked, and good-looking girl of about my own age, in a green-checked tartan plaid. I should have left them to go home along the beach, while they took their

way over the hills; but I got to log-gerheads with the oldest one about her "expecting to ride some day in her carriage," when I went with them by the high road as far as the old Cruicks' farm-house, "arguing the question," and stood there for some time doing it. This was my first ex-perience of what is called "female pertinacity," for I could make noth-ing of her in the way of argument, al-though it was doubtless "mere asser-tion" on both sides. I almost came to blows with her before parting, and went home completely discomfited. There I pestered every one for sym-pathy, and harped on the words, "To think o' a muckle, coarse-looking jad like that riding in her carriage!"

At the Ferry there was an old-es-tablished company or association of boatmen that might have been called a close corporation, before the intro-duction of steam. In my father's work on the Gipsies (which I edited and published in 1865), there is the following in reference to them:—

"So well did they [the Gipsies] pay their way at the village and passage alluded to, that the boatmen gave them the kindly name of 'our frien's.' These wanderers were all known at the village by the name of 'Gillie Wheesels,' or 'Killie Wheesh,' which in the west of Fife signified 'the lads that take the purses.' Old Thomas Chalmers informed me that he had frequently seen these sharks of boat-men shake these Gipsy thieves heart-ily by the hand, and, with a signifi-cant smile on their harsh, weather-beaten countenances, wish them a good market as they landed them on the north side of the Forth, on their way to picking pockets at fairs" (p. 173).

Before the introduction of a steam ferry-boat, these boatmen had things pretty much their own way; for at-tempts had been made to employ other boatmen, which failed, in con-sequence of their not being familiar with the tides and currents in the gut between the ferries. In my rec-ollection there was still some little boating done there, while the men perhaps eked out a living by fishing. They were frequently seen loitering about the light-house. The only one that I particularly noticed was a queer-looking little body, called "Daft W—— G——"; but he was not so "daft" as not to know what to do with a pocket-book containing bank notes which he found, for it was reported that he "burned the book, but kept the bonnie pictures."

The only "business man" living at the Ferry was the one who leased the Ferry Hills, and was extensively connected with the mail service and posting, and kept the inn, as mentioned (p. 55). He was a very active, enterprising, and successful man, and was well known far and wide, and well liked. In his manner he was pushing and energetic and popular, and was quite a "character." It was alleged that he would enter his stable and kindly slap his horses and descant on their merits. To one he said, "Ay, you have earned me £200." I once heard him say that when he was young he did not rest a moment after awaking in the morning, but instantly gathered his bed-clothes on his feet and threw them over the end of his bed, and sprung to the floor. These were two distinct movements, but so active was he in after-life that in his youth they might almost have passed for one.

There was another "character" living at the Ferry, but often seen in Inverkeithing, who bore the title of Captain, from having been a sailing-master in the navy, as I always understood, although in the neighbourhood any one who had held a commission seems to have been styled Captain by courtesy. Although pretty-well advanced in life and hardly straight in his figure, he was active in his habits, springy in his movements, and buoyant in his manners. He took the first place in suggesting all kinds of improvements. In every way he was an object of public interest and even admiration, as a "wonderful body," and when he met with a serious accident—the breakage of one or both legs, or some such misfortune—the feeling was that "that was the end of him"; but he "got on his legs" as before. Most of his dress was in the pink of almost youthful fashion, with a broad-brimmed beaver hat that inclined a little towards his shoulders, and from under it hung a queue or pigtail, while opposite that was a 'countenance that was not very imposing in its aspect. I recollect my father pointing out a narrow close at the Ferry, in which the Captain had an adventure. He had gone there to make peace between a woman and her wild and drunken husband, when the ruffian roared and rushed for his gun, and the Captain made for the door, but, instead of running straight out of the close, threw or "wapped" himself from side to side till he twisted himself round the entrance of it, so as not to give his assailant (whether real or pretended) a good aim at him. In that respect he followed the regulation tactics observed when retreating, pell-mell, in narrow streets. A son of the Captain on returning to Leith, after a residence in England, said, "How do you people in Scotland keep your holidays at Christmas?" "Just as they do at the North Queensferry, where I have been many a day," was the reply of a person present, who was also a native of the place.

During Bonaparte's wars my father was a lieutenant in the volunteer artillery stationed at the North Queensferry. I recollect him pointing out where the guns were placed. There were two batteries; one along the edge of the cliff that encircled the village on the east of it, and one on a small low-lying piece or point of land outside of the pier that formed the eastern side of the little harbour. This battery had consisted of but two guns, with earth forming three small mounds to protect them at the sides only. This light earth-work had kept its appearance wonderfully. Everything relating to the high battery, which had doubtless been of a more extensive, heavier, and more solid nature than the other one, had disappeared. My father's commission, epaulets, sash, and sword were well taken care of, but his coat—I think blue with red trimmings—and hat were allowed to go to ruin.

In my time the only recently-built houses at the Ferry were the inn and the school-house at the top of the hill. The inn was a handsome building, having its back so close to the water that it seemed to form part of the sea-line. Its inmates had thus the most convenient facilities for bathing. The school-house was of two stories ; the full length of the under one for the school-room, and the upper one for the teachers' dwelling, which was entered by a stair from the north side. The windows differed from ordinary ones, being of the "cottage" order, or of some such description. In the school-room in the evenings there was frequently. preaching, which seems to have differed from what was heard from the "Old Moderate" in the parish church. I always went there cheerfully except on one occasion, when, a little before starting for the place, I had the misfortune to fall into the sea, at the east side of the Lazaretto wall, and wet myself to the knees, but not while "gathering sticks," which was rigidly prohibited on Sundays. I said nothing of the occurrence, but started for church, while I felt most anxious for a change of clothing ; but it being in the height of summer, the disagreeable feeling and the danger were considerably modified. The only oldish building at the Ferry (excepting the old inn) that I took particular notice of, was a heavy-looking house facing the street, with its back to the sea, on the right as the village was entered from the west. In it resided an old gentleman who had been my father's ranking officer in the volunteer artillery.

While loitering about the Ferry till nearly dark, before the time of steam, my father noticed a post-chaise arrive from the north in gallant style. Out of it came a young man in the highest fashion, and took his departure for the south side, on his way to Edinburgh, in a ferry-boat that sank deep in the water with some heavy trunks that formed his luggage. After thinking over what he had seen, my father hired a boat and reported the circumstance to the Customs' authorities at Leith ; when next day the trunks were traced and seized, but not before some marks had been removed from the bottom of them. It turned out that they contained costly British lace, an article that had been frequently exported by a Leith mercantile house to Holland, in the face of Bonaparte's Berlin decrees, prohibiting trade with Great Britain ; to counteract which the British Government granted licenses to import free of duty, goods to the same value that were landed in Holland. The removal of the marks from the trunks ended the investigation ; for in smuggling, as in murder, the goods must be produced and identified before an action can hold. Up to this time the mercantile house alluded to had been very successful in exporting lace (always lace, that was very valuable and easily handled) and importing the value of it, free of duty, as mentioned, and producing certificates of the lace having been landed in Holland, to the astonishment and envy of their neighbours. But their trade at once ceased and was never resumed. A singular circumstance connected with the subject was, that the searcher who cleared the trunks for export found in one of them a pen which he had lost on the day he did it ; but that was not deemed sufficient evidence. It was believed that a fishing boat had run alongside of the vessel below the island of Inchkeith, and landed the trunks on the Fife coast, from which they were taken to Edinburgh in the way described. In that case it was possible that the same trunks, or the lace contained in them, had been the basis of many profitable Dutch adventures. Had the marks on the trunks not been removed (which was probably done before they left the vessel), my father would doubtless have received a "nice sum" for his services.

I bring these "Reminiscences of Childhood at Inverkeithing" to a close by saying that, after seeing the *Esperance* leave the Lazaretto pier with our furniture for Leith, the family scattered, and passed their last night in the neighbourhood among friends and relations. I went with my three sisters to an uncle of my father at Limekilns. He was the out-port deputy-collector or coast-officer of the Custom-house at Bo'ness, and dwelt in the eastern one of two houses at the foot of a hill, a little west of the pier, and nearly opposite an ancient structure on the sea-shore, of the nature of which I could never learn. It was of heavy stone, and might have been the well of salt-pans that had long ceased to exist, and looked as if it had been at least three centuries old. The business of the district seemed to be at Charlestown,

immediately to the west, for of the pier at Limekilns I might say that I never saw a vessel near it, except the "bones of an old sloop," or some such craft, that had been drawn up alongside of it as far as it could be floated at the highest tide. We spent a night of great hilarity in the house of a kindly and worthy old man, of limited education and capacity, but in appearance, manners, and character of a high order. Early next day we embarked at Charlestown for Newhaven in a little steam-tug called the *Lion*—which was painted black, white, and green, and "clinker-built"¹ —and picked up the rest of the family at the Ferry. Although the weather was wet, I got a good view of what was to be seen on our side of St. Margaret's Hope, including the guard-ship, the ruins of Rosyth Castle and St. Margaret's, and after these, of the Ferry and Caroline's Nose, and enjoyed the novelty of seeing familiar places from a point outside of them. After fairly passing the Ferry, and getting a good sight of the island of Inchgarvie, I cast many a look along the coast towards the Lazaretto and Inverkeithing. When these became indistinct, as we advanced towards our new home, I bade them adieu, but not for ever.

APPENDIX.

WITH reference to the *History of the Gipsies*, I have said in the Preface, that " it is partly in relation to this work that I have prepared these Reminiscences, as alluded to in the Appendix." I sent the book home in 1865, with the idea that it would at least be treated fairly by the Scotch press generally; but it seems that the most part of it declined to notice it in any way, while not a single publication discussed it with reference to the really important aspect of the subject—the development of the race as its blood became mixed with native, and its members took their places, more or less, in the ranks of settled life, in common with the other inhabitants. Indeed there seems to have been an aversion even to touch the work, or the subject of it, in any way, were I to judge by the very favourable notice of it in the *Edinburgh Weekly Herald*, in which, after much apparent hesitation or " swithering," it began thus :—" This, let us say it at once." I can only conjecture in regard to the reason for this, for I am not in a position to make a specific charge against anyone for what I cannot but consider a dereliction of duty. A book of such a nature, originating as this one did, on being returned to Scotland, was entitled to be received there with the greatest courtesy and candour; for such is not a thing of every-day occurrence, that can be passed over as a matter of indifference. I admit that the popular feeling against the very name of Gipsy is such that it is with the utmost difficulty, or barely possible, attention can be arrested for almost anything good or sensible in regard to it. But that was no reason why the subject, as treated in this book, should have been proscribed, in the face of the evidence furnished in relation to it.

To intelligent and disinterested people it should appear intuitively and instinctively, that the hard feeling on the part of the world at large against the Gipsy race results in the following positions :—

1st. Our knowing so little of the Gipsies in general, and absolutely nothing of them when, by dropping their original habits, and keeping silent on the subject, they " cease to be Gipsies " in popular estimation.

2d. Separation in their feelings, private associations, and marriages from the community at large ; and a corresponding perpetuation of their existence as Gipsies or members of the Gipsy tribe.

3d. A natural feeling of antipathy, whether active or passive, on the part of the Gipsies towards the rest of the population.

4th. The moral impossibility of the race, as a rule, marrying with and " amalgamating and becoming lost " among the natives, when they have never been allowed by them even to " open their mouths " as Gipsies.

5th. That the Gipsy element, whether pure in regard to blood (of the existence of which there is great doubt) or mixed, or even common blood " gipsified," will also *naturally* marry with the Gipsy element, and thereby perpetuate itself, as a tribe, or a community in the midst of another, by a law of nature, as much as that by which other races or families of men are preserved distinct from others.

6th. That habits or character, calling or creed, do not enter into the question of a person being a member of a race springing from a tent, that entered Scotland not later than 1506, and England in the time of Henry VIII., and that has a knowledge or belief of its existence all over the world.

7th. That no one should object to a person claiming to be, and being in fact, a member of this race, and priding himself in it, in the face of the ferocity of prejudice against it, while he, on his part, claims the privilege of being a member of a particular native family, or of an association that is in any way separated from the rest of the population : seeing that the first is such pre-eminently by a law of nature and social pressure, and not by choice ; and the second mainly by family records, while as a member of an association he is such entirely by choice.

With these remarks, I ask, What were the objections to the *History of the Gipsies?* It referred to a people living in Scotland, and was a purely Scotch question, in which every " patriot" was supposed to be interested. Did anyone know that what was contained in the work was not true ? If he did, then it was his duty to have exposed it. If he knew or believed that it was true, it was also his duty to have admitted it, and done justice to it. If he did not know whether it was true or not, he should have had it investigated and discussed, and admitted if true, or rejected if false. If he had asked himself what reason he had for objecting to what was published as truth, he would have found it difficult to frame an intelligible answer to the question. He could not have referred to a much better authority than himself; and he could hardly have *said* (whatever he might have *felt*) that he objected to what was given as facts merely because he " chose to do so."

In *The Scottish Churches and the Gipsies* I said that " the social emancipation of the Gipsies is in reality a turning-point in history" (p. 24). But in treating the question the first thing to be done is to investigate and understand it, and intelligibly realize the fact that the race is not confined to the few that go about, somewhat in the more primitive condition of it.

Here there is no room for prejudices, preconceived opinions or precedents, or any other motives bearing on the investigation of truth, whatever may have been the conventional light in which it may have been looked at heretofore. What becomes of the Gipsies as they (or the representatives of the blood) disappear from view, is simply a subject of investigation, in which common sense and fair play should be shown. And yet, instead of confining the inquiry exclusively to the race itself, people are very apt to " go off at a tangent " in regard to some other one ; forgetting that the Jewish and Gipsy elements of society are the only apparent exceptions to the rule of absorption of foreign blood in the British population, as I have illustrated at great length, in the *Disquisition on the Gipsies,* in regard to the descendants of people from other parts of Europe becoming British subjects by " mere birth and rearing on the soil." But although they thus become " British," that is not the whole of the question. For even when two people from different towns in Scotland have children born to them and reared in another town in Scotland, the issue have the feelings of being natives of that town, as much as those whose ancestors lived in it " for time out of mind," but retain a sense of belonging to a particular family or connection, whatever the quarter to which they may trace it. And if we admit that, cannot we easily realize, in a much greater degree, the same of a Gipsy family, which is of such a recent addition to the Scotch population, when it has not only never been acknowledged, but has been legally and socially proscribed, so that they have carefully and rigidly kept a knowledge of it to themselves, as if they had had to "skulk through life like thieves, conspirators or assassins, afraid of being apprehended by all they meet with, in the event of these coming to learn all about them, however good their characters may be?"—*Contributions, etc.,* p. 202.

So far from the Gipsies (whatever the occasional exceptions) getting "mixed and lost" among the natives, a certain part of the native blood has got "mixed and lost" among them; having had the effect of greatly adding to their number, modifying their appearance, and facilitating their disappearance, *to the eye,* among the rest of the population. Under any circumstances it should not be maintained, without investigation and proof, that the Gipsy element has been "lost," merely because it relieves the public of the trouble and responsibility of discharging its duty in regard to the race, in the various stages of its development after dropping, for the most part, the outward peculiarities of the original representatives of it. As illustrative of what I have said, I give the following from the *Spectator,* of so recent a date as the 22d October, 1881 :—

"If Gipsies could be induced to settle in England, as they have been in Scotland, where roamers are now very few, they would have to work, and would soon be absorbed in the surrounding population."

The English language is surely capable of defining more accurately the destiny of the Gipsy element in society, as it settles and divests itself of what is outwardly characteristic of it in its primitive condition, than to say that it thereby becomes "absorbed in the surrounding population." I could hardly have thought that a journal of the standing of the *Spectator* could have used such language, after all that I had written on the subject and submitted to it, unless it appears that this "absorption" theory is so absolutely conventional that no one must call it in question, however much it may be demonstrated to have no foundation in fact. It must be obvious to anyone that even an ordinary native does not get "absorbed" in the population of London by taking up his residence in it ; although it might be said, in a general way, that he gets "lost" in it, that is, he loses his self-importance, and makes it a difficult matter to find him. All the influences bearing on the destiny of the Gipsies—those that originate within themselves and those that press upon them from without—should surely lead to a conclusion different from the one in vogue. We have had elaborate treatises on all kinds of subjects, including cats and insects, and might have them on the mechanism of butterflies' wings—all more or less interesting, in common with whatever society directs its attention to ; and yet it seems difficult to get a common-sense theory adopted, and the facts received, in regard to a people that appeared in England so recently as the time of Henry VIII., particularly in reference to the principles of its existence and destiny, as *it* absorbs the native blood, and contemplates all outside of the circle of its sympathy, which embraces a relatively-large number of people in the British Isles.

It was with the object of directing attention to the *History of the Gipsies,* and to my addition to the subject of it, that I lately sent by mail a great many copies of a pamphlet, entitled *The English Universities and John Bunyan,* to the press in Great

Britain and Ireland, the universities, English great high schools, and the bishops and deans. Shortly after that I distributed in the same way four hundred copies of a publication entitled *The Scottish Churches and the Gipsies*, which contained the preceding one and some other matter relating to the Gipsies and the Jews. Of these I sent a copy to each of the presbytery clerks of the three Presbyterian Churches in Scotland, the British and Irish universities, the English great high schools, and the bishops and deans, and one of the canons, " and for the perusal by courtesy of the other canons." I adopted this course, to bring the subject before the university men of England, for the reasons given in the pamphlet specially addressed to them ; and yet I find the *Saturday Review*, on the occasion of a meeting of the Archæological Institute at Bedford, writing, on the 17th September, 1881, as follows :—

" Mr. Brown showed that, so far from Bunyan being of Gipsy descent, as an ingenious American writer has endeavoured to prove, the name Bunyan, in one of its many forms, had been already known in Bedfordshire for full seven centuries."

I had an article, published in *Notes and Queries*, of the 27th March, 1875, and reprinted in *Contributions, etc.*, in 1875, and in *The Scottish Churches and the Gipsies*, in 1881, showing very fully the unreasonableness of maintaining that John Bunyan could *not* have been a Gipsy because the name Bunyan (variously spelt) was in existence in England before the Gipsies arrived there. In that article I wrote as follows :—

" The tradition among all the British Gipsies is that their British names were originally assumed from those of people of influence, among whom the tribe settled, as they scattered over the country, and had districts assigned to them, under chieftains, with a king over all, and tokens or passes to keep each in his district, or from infringing on the rights of other families. All that is

fully explained in *Simson's History of the Gipsies* (pp. 116, 117, 205 and 218), where will also be found (p. 206) the fancy the tribe have always had for terming themselves ' braziers,' and having the word put on their tombstones." (*Con.*, p. 185). And that " John Bunyan could not possibly have been a Gipsy, for the reason that others of the British race were of the same name ! and, as a corollary, that no one bearing a British name can, under any circumstances, be a Gipsy !" (p. 184).

Let us consider this subject as one of law between two parties ; one clamorously calling on the judge and jury to give him possession of an estate on the strength of his *name*, without regard to his *pedigree*, and absolutely refusing to allow the real evidence to be laid before the court, in regard to the rightful heir. Of the two writers (the Rev. John Brown, of Bunyan Meeting, and one in the *Sunday Magazine*), who put torth the illusion that the *name* settles the question of Bunyan *not* having been a Gipsy, I wrote in the article alluded to, thus :—

" The two gentlemen mentioned seem to know very little, if anything, of the subject, and should have exhausted every source of information, and looked at every side of the question, before so dogmatically asserting that they ' do away with the supposition of those who think that John Bunyan may have had Gipsy blood in his veins ' ; that ' the idea of Bunyan being of Gipsy race, is totally discountenanced ' ; and that the long existence of the name in the county, ' effectually disposes of the supposition that the Bunyans were Gipsies ' " (p. 184).

The real evidence in regard to Bunyan's pedigree and nationality is to be found in what he told us of himself, in *Grace Abounding*, as follows :—

" For my descent, it was, *as is well known to many*, of a low and inconsiderable generation, my father's house being of that rank that is *meanest and most despised* of *all* the families in the land."—" Another thought came into my mind, and that was, whether we [his family and relations] were of the Israelites or no ; for finding in the Scriptures that they were once the peculiar people of God, thought I, if I were one of this race [how significant is the expression !] my soul must needs be happy. Now, again, I found within 'me a great longing to be resolved about this question, but could not tell how I should. At last I asked my father of it, who told me, No, we [his father included] were not."*

I have not been able to see Mr. Brown's book (although I wrote for it), and cannot therefore say whether he attempted to give an explanation of Bunyan's account of himself, in regard to what he *was* and *was not*, or entirely ignored it. Having raised the question about his pedigree or nationality, he should have " exhausted every source of information " before even attempting to decide it ; but he seems to have wilfully disregarded everything bearing on the subject. In that respect I have said that

" The name of Bunyan having been borne by native families would not, under any circumstances, even make it probable that John Bunyan was *not* a Gipsy, for there is a great variety of native names among the race. Had he belonged to the native race, he could have said that he was, in all probability, of a ' fine old Saxon family in reduced circumstances, related to a baronet and many respectable families ' " (p. 185), or of one that entered England with William the Conqueror !

* Bunyan adds :—" But, notwithstanding the meanness and inconsiderableness of my parents, it pleased God to put it into their hearts to put me to school, to learn both to read and write ; the which I also attained, according to the rate of other poor men's children."—He does not say, " according to the rate of poor men's children," but of "*other* poor men's children " : a form of expression always used by the Gipsies when speaking of themselves, as distinguished from others. The language of Bunyan, in speaking of his family, was in harmony with that of the population at large ; but he, doubtless, had the feelings peculiar to all the tribe, in reference to their origin and race.—*Disquisition*, p. 511.

Even in regard to solid English farmers of to-day, no one would ever think of saying that a tinker (whatever his pedigree) was necessarily, or under any circumstances, a brother or a cousin of them, merely on account of the similarity of the surname, and his frequenting or living in their neighbourhood, or having been born in it. And no more reason would there be for saying the same in 1628, when Bunyan was born. Between 1506, when the Gipsies arrived in Great Britain, and 1628, I have said that " there had doubtless been six generations of the race born in the land "; so that there had been ample time for it, in its mixture of blood, to have settled and advanced so far as it did to the birth of the immortal dreamer.*

The question at issue is really not

* At the meeting at Bedford alluded to, Mr. Brown is reported as having said :—
" The Bunyans of Elstow—where they were living as early as 1603—appear to have been the poor retainers of a family other branches of which were substantial yeomen in the county quite three centuries ago." The expression " poor retainers of a family " would imply that John Bunyan's family were a broken-down branch of one of the English aristocracy, titled or untitled ; whereas, as we have seen, Bunyan himself said that his "father's house," in point of " rank," was of " the meanest and most despised of *all* the families in the land," and that they were *not Jews*.
Mr. Brown says (and in this respect he is apparently correct) that the father and grandfather of John Bunyan were called Thomas ; and that the former was baptized at Elstow Church on the —— February, 1603, and married on the 23d May, 1627, to his *second* wife, Margaret Bentley, the mother of John Bunyan, who was baptized at Elstow on the 30th November, 1628. There are doubtless other records and other information bearing on the *name* Bunyan, which Mr. Brown has withheld from the world. For example, is nothing said of the *callings* and *residences* of the fathers of Thomas Bunyan and Margaret Bentley in the entry of the marriage ?
The *Saturday Review* further said that " even Dean Merivale had to devote several paragraphs of his address to the

one of evidence, but of an unfortunate feeling of caste, and the aversion that many have to change their opinions, particularly in regard to those alluded to in the preface, who are not given to research or original thought, and have not " the mental flexibility that enables others to look back and forward, and throw themselves into positions besides those they had been long and carefully trained to fill"; saying nothing of those who, " 'caring for none of these things,' are for the most part engrossed in their callings, and the amenities connected with their positions in life." The subject is one of vital importance and interest, although society, from whatever cause, seems to be indisposed to entertain it.

In *Contributions to Natural History*, etc., I wrote as follows :—

" Nor could it be almost imagined that, in a constitutional country, in a time of peace, with the courts in full operation, any question that is actionable should be denied even a hearing by a competent court, on the plea of favouring the defendant . . . . or to gratify popular prejudices against a suit

---

local hero," speaking of him as almost " the patron saint, the pride and glory of the town, the famous John Bunyan "; and yet he did not acknowledge him, but maintained, or allowed it to be said, in spite of evidence, that in regard to his *race* he was what he was *not.* Long before the meeting I sent the Dean a copy of the pamphlets entitled *The English Universities and John Bunyan* and *The Scottish Churches and the Gipsies.* The *Saturday Review,* as we have seen, indirectly acknowledged the copy of the former, which was sent to it.

The whole trouble or mystery in regard to Bunyan is solved by the simple idea of a Gipsy family settling in the neighbourhood of native families of influence, whose surname they assumed, and making Elstow their headquarters or residence, as was the uniform custom of the tribe all over Great Britain. This circumstance makes it a difficult matter, in some instances, to distinguish, by the Christian and surnames in county parish registers, " which was which," so far back as the early part of the seventeenth century.

that is legal and moral in its nature. The same may be said of the laws and courts of *criticism ;* for if they are in a sound state they will at once entertain, discuss and settle any and every question suitable to the journal before which it is brought. It is unquestionably within their sphere to entertain *demurrers,* and see that they are respected, to the extent at least that no one can be allowed to make assertions, and assertions only, after they have been repeatedly denied, with proofs of denial, or arguments showing them to be untenable, or highly improbable. They should also see that no denial or assertion is permitted unless it is accompanied by evidence, or an argument in its favour " (p. 204).

" It is a law in literature, indeed it is common sense, that if nothing can be said in favour of one of two hypotheses, and everything in favour of the other, the latter must be accepted as the truth ; and this we have in the one that Bunyan was a Gipsy. All that is wanting to change the hypothesis into a fact would be Bunyan's verbal acknowledgment, which the legal and social proscription of the race and name would prevent him making, and which strengthens the Gipsy hypothesis as such; so that if we have not his *formal* confession, we have his *inferential* admission, as *circumstantial* evidence, which is better than assertion either way, when a man's estate, character, or life is at stake " (p. 202).

As to John Bunyan not having been a Gipsy, but an ordinary native of England, there is not a particle of evidence to show it ; for which reason it should never be maintained by sensible and self-respecting men. On the other hand, the proof in favour of his having been a member of the Gipsy tribe is complete, for it was not necessary that he should have used the word in the face of the legal and social responsibility attaching to it ; the latter of which is apparently as great to-day as it was in Bunyan's time. In the *Disquisition on the Gipsies* I said that " John Bunyan has told us as much of his history *as he dared to do*" (p. 516); and that " in mentioning that much of himself which he did, Bunyan doubtless imagined that the world understood, or would have understood, what he meant, and would, sooner or later, acknowledge the race to which he belonged" (p. 517). And in regard to matters of fact generally, I have said, that "if it is wrong to believe that to be a truth which has never been investigated, it becomes culpable to enunciate it as such" (*Con.*, p. 204).

By receiving John Bunyan as a Gipsy, I said in *Contributions, etc.*, that

"Settling this question in the affirmative would resemble a decision in a supreme court of justice in a case that is representative of many others ; and could not fail to have an immense influence on the raising up of the Gipsy tribe, to which Bunyan belonged " (p. 203),

whether it applied to the more primitive members of the race or to those differing in no *outward* respect from the rest of the population.

In regard to this subject, what I wrote in *Contributions, etc.*, in 1878, is equally applicable to 1882 :—

"It would also be strange to have it said that, in the year 1878, the British press, religious or secular, would not tolerate the idea that John Bunyan was a Gipsy even to appear in its columns ; and that people frowned upon or became fired with indignation at the bare mention of it, while they wondered that, if it were so, Bunyan should not have told us plainly of the fact, when it was odious to the rest of the population, and death by law for being a Gipsy, and 'felony without benefit of clergy' for associating with the race, or even being found in its company " (p. 203).

What I have said of the *Spectator* and the *Saturday Review*, detracts somewhat from the following passage in regard to a part of the English press :—

"Still, in England, there is that sense of dignity and honourable dealing among high-class, high-toned journals, that if they do not entertain or do justice to the book (or rather to the subjects discussed in it), they will not abuse it. And,

besides that, there is a strong conservative feeling peculiar to most of them that impels them to be careful in regard to what they introduce to their readers ; which is a great drawback to anything novel or original, whatever its truth or attraction, being given to the world through their pages " (p. 205).*

This feeling of conservative conventionalism has been characteristic of man in all ages, and under almost all circumstances ; and has frequently strewn the ground leading to the advance of knowledge with every hateful passion. Conventionalism, in some form, is an essential element· in society, or rather constitutes it, however it may change ; and

---

* In what I have published I seem to have incurred the ill-will of the *Scotsman:* It spoke of the "pretentious absurdity" of the title of the *History of the Gipsies*, a book of 575 closely printed pages ; and said that it was "worse than calling a school an academy to take a number of loose notes upon the Gipsies of Scotland, to add to them a few looser notes upon Gipsies in general, and then to entitle the volume a history of that remarkable people."—In its critique on *Contributions to Natural History, etc.*, copied at page 206 in the second edition of it, it said :—" The puzzle is, why he should suppose that his views . . . . are of the smallest importance to any human being except himself." Its notice of *The Scottish Churches and the Gipsies*, on the 22d December, 1881, read as follows :—" All that can be positively asserted about the strange olla-podrida which Mr. James Simson has put together under the title, *The Scottish Churches and the Gipsies*, is that it contains a great deal of rambling writing about the Gipsies, and next to nothing about the Scottish Churches, or their attitude towards the ' Romany Rye.' Mr. Simson is one of those troublesome persons who think that they know everything, some pet subject ; and nobody else anything, about that anybody who presumes to treat that subject without studying and accepting as gospel what they have written upon it, is guilty of a crime of the deepest dye ; and that their petty literary squabbles are deserving of elaborate record. This book is an embodiment of Mr. Simson's idiosyncrasies in a very pronounced form. No more cruel penalty could be inflicted on the author's worst literary foe than to be condemned to read it through."

is a great good in itself, provided that it does not last too long or go too far, and is accompanied by the courtesy and candour that open the way to the entertainment, discussion, and reception of truth, whatever it may refer to. As regards social intercourse, it is indispensable in civilized communities, and manifests itself more or less among savage and barbarous races, especially in relation to their religious or superstitious observances. Among civilized people, after many a battle, conventional beliefs, with little or no real investigation, may be said to be the mental condition of human nature; for which reason, if one's knowledge is limited to what is merely current, however much he may have been trained in it, or however much he may have acquired of it, it may still be said that, in the absence of originality of mind, he is little more than a "commonplace personage," and often a "bar in the way" to the development of every form of truth.

As regards the subject of the Gipsy race, what is aimed at is to establish that which should have been settled in the time of Henry VIII., "particularly in reference to the principles of its existence and destiny, as it absorbs the native blood, and contemplates all outside of the circle of its sympathy" (p. 79). On this subject assertions have been made, and may yet be made, without regard to investigation and proof, by people interesting themselves in it; in regard to some of whom, whatever their positions in life, there is no evidence of their non-connection with the tribe, and of their not playing on words, or not writing in good faith.

I have spent too much money, and have had too much trouble, in connection with this matter; and it is time, after this and previous appeals to those living in Great Britain, that it should be taken off my hands. Personally it has hitherto almost appeared that one who is absent from his native country has no rights in it. Britons should have that much good sense as to see that if they keep up their prejudice (the only one they have in regard to race) against the Gipsies (so far, at least, as the name is concerned), they will not acknowledge themselves, excepting those who cannot help it, and who live by being such; and that much love of country and humanity as not to allow this race, or name, to remain in the position it has hitherto done. Moreover, they should not permit it to be said that any of their battles should be fought exclusively by one of themselves (and at his expense), thirty years absent, and three thousand miles distant from them; or that they shirk responsibilities of any kind.

I add a few extracts from the *Disquisition on the Gipsies* (published in 1865), bearing on the leading features of the race after leaving the tent, and conforming, more or less, with the ways of the other inhabitants.

I am afraid that what has been said is not sufficiently explanatory to enable some people to understand this subject. These people know what a Gipsy, in the popular sense, means; they have either seen him and observed his general mode of life, or had the same described to them in books. This idea of a Gipsy has been impressed upon their minds almost from infancy. But it puzzles most people to form any idea of a Gipsy of a higher order; such a Gipsy, for example, as preaches the Gospel, or argues the law: that seems, hitherto, to have been almost incomprehensible to them. They know intuitively what is meant by any particular people who occupy a territory—any country, tract of land, or isle. They also know what is meant by the existence of the Jews. For the subject is familiar to them from infancy; it is wrapt up in their early reading; it is associated with the knowledge and practice of their religion, and the attendance, on the part of the Jews, at a place of worship. They have likewise seen and conversed with the Jews, or others who have done either or both; or they are acquainted with them by the current remarks of the world. But a people resembling, in so many respects, the Jews, without having any territory, or form of creed, peculiar to itself, or any history, or any peculiar outward associations or residences, or any material difference in appearance, character, or occupation, is something that the general mind of mankind would seem never to have dreamt of, or to be almost capable of realizing to itself (p. 447).

Take a Gipsy in his original state, and we can find nothing really *vulgar* about him. . . . . He does not consider himself as belonging to the same race as the native, and would rather be judged by a different standard. The life which he leads is not that of the lowest class of the country in which he dwells, but the primitive, original state of a people of great antiquity, proscribed by law and society; himself an enemy of, and an enemy to, all around him; with the population so prejudiced against him, that attempts to change his condition, consistently with his feelings as a man, are frequently in vain; so that, on the ground of strict morals, or even administrative justice, the man can be said to be only half responsible. The subject, however, assumes quite a different aspect when we consider a Gipsy of education and refinement, like the worthy clergyman mentioned, between whose condition and that of his tented ancestor an interval of, perhaps, two or three centuries has elapsed. We should then put him on the footing of any other race having a barbarous origin, and entertain no prejudice against him on account of the race to which he belongs. . . . . I would place such a Gipsy on the footing of the Hungarian race; with this difference, that the Hungarians entered Europe in the ninth century, and became a people, occupying a territory; while the Gipsies appeared in the fifteenth century, and are now to be found, civilized and uncivilized, in almost every corner of the known world (p. 414).—That the Gipsies were a barbarous race when they entered Europe, in the beginning of the fifteenth century, is just what could have been expected of any Asiatic, migratory, tented horde, at a time when the inhabitants of Europe were little better than barbarous themselves, and many of them absolutely so (p. 465).

As a wandering, barbarous, tented

tribe, with habits peculiar to itself, and inseparable from its very nature, great allowance ought to be made for its gradual absorption into settled society.* That could only be the result of generations, even if the race had not been treated so harshly as it has been, or had such a prejudice displayed against it. The difficulties which a Gipsy has to encounter in leaving the tent are great, for he has been born in that state, and been reared in it. . . . . Then there is the prejudice of the world—the objection to receive him into any community, and his children into any school — that commonly prevails, and which compels him to *steal* into settled life. It has always been so with the Gipsy race. Gipsies brought up in the tent have the same difficulties to encounter in leaving it to-day that others had centuries ago. But, notwithstanding all that, they are always keeping moving out of the tent, and becoming settled and civilized (p. 482).

It requires no argument to show that there is no tribe or nation but finds something that leads it to cling to its origin and descent, and not despise the blood that runs in its own veins, although it may despise the condition or conduct of some of its members. Where shall we find an exception to this rule? The Gipsy race is no exception to it. Civilize a Gipsy, and you make him a civilized Gipsy; educate him, and you make him an educated Gipsy.; bring him up to any profession you like, Christianize him as much as you may, and he still remains a Gipsy; because he is of the Gipsy race, and all the influences of nature and revelation do not affect the questions of blood, tribe, and nationality (p. 412).—The principle of progression, the passing through one phase of history into another, while the race maintains its identity, holds good with the Gipsies, as well as with any other people (p. 414).—By bringing up the body in the manner done in this work, by making a sweep of the whole tribe, the responsibility becomes spread over a large number of people; so that, should

* I have said, "absorption into *settled society*"; a very different idea from "getting lost among the rest of the population," as is popularly believed, without investigation or knowledge of the subject.

the Gipsy become by any means known personally to the world, he would have the satisfaction of knowing that he had others to keep him company ; men occupying respectable positions in life, and respected by the world at large as individuals (p. 465).

In their wild state, they have never been charged by anyone with an outward contempt for religion, whatever their inward feelings may have been for it ; but, on the contrary, as always having shown an apparent respect for it. No one has ever complained of the Gipsy scoffing at religion, or even for not yielding to its general truths ; what has been said of him is, that he is, at heart, so heedless and volatile in his disposition, that everything in regard to religion passes in at the one ear and goes out at the other. . . . . As regards the question of religion, it is very fortunate for the Gipsy race that they brought no particular one with them ; for, objectionable as they have been held to be, the feeling towards them would have been worse if they had had a system of priestcraft and heathen idolatry among them. But this circumstance greatly worries a respectable Gipsy ; he would much rather have it said that his ancestors had some sort of religion, than that they had none (p. 477).—It is the weak position which the Gipsy race occupies in the world, as it enters upon a settled life and engages in steady pursuits, that compels it to assume an incognito ; for it has nothing to appeal to as regards the past ; no history, except it be acts of legislation passed against the race. In looking into a dictionary or a cyclopædia, the Gipsy finds his race described as vagabonds, always as vagabonds ; and he may be said never to have heard a good word spoken of it, during the whole of his life. Hence he and his descendants " keep as quiet as pussy," and pass from the observation of the world. Besides this, there is no prominent feature connected with his race, to bring it before the world, such as there is with the Jewish, viz :—history, church or literature (p. 480).

In the descent of a native family, in the instance given, the issue follows the name of the family. But, with the Gipsy race, the thing to be transmitted is not merely a question of family, but a race distinct from any particular family (p. 451).—When the Gipsies emerge from their original condition, they occupy as good positions in the world as the Jews ; while they have about them none of those outward peculiarities of the Jews that make them, in a manner, offensive to other people. In every sense but that of belonging to the Gipsy tribe, they are ordinary natives ; for the circumstances that have formed the characters of the ordinary natives have formed theirs. . . . . Indeed one will naturally look for certain superior points of character in a man who has fairly emerged from a wild and barbarous state, which he will not be apt to find in another who has fallen from a higher position in the scale of nations (p. 500). —For this reason, it must be said of the race, that whenever it shakes itself clear of objectionable habits, and follows any kind of ordinary industry, the cause of every prejudice against it is gone, or ought to disappear ; for then, as I have already said, the Gipsies become ordinary citizens, of the Gipsy clan (p. 479).—The Gipsy, as he emerges from his wild state, makes ample amends for his original offensiveness, by hiding everything relative to his being a Gipsy from his neighbours around him (p. 483).

What are the respectable, well-disposed Scottish Gipsies but Scotch people, after all ? . They are to be met with in almost every, if not every, sphere in which the ordinary Scot is to be found. The only difference between the two is, that, however mixed the blood of these Gipsies may be, their associations of descent and tribe go back to those black, mysterious heroes who entered Scotland, upwards of three hundred and fifty years ago ; and that, with this descent, they have the words and signs of Gipsies. The possession of all these, with the knowledge of the feelings which the ordinary natives have for the very name of Gipsy, makes the only distinction between them and other Scotchmen. I do not say that the world would have any prejudice against these Gipsies, as Gipsies ; still they are morbidly sensitive that it would have such a feeling (p. 437).—As for the other part of the race—those whose habits are unexceptionable—it is for us to convince them that no prejudice is entertained for them on account of their being Gipsies ; but that it would rather be pleasing and interesting for us to know something of them as Gipsies, that is, about their feelings as Gipsies, and hear them talk some of this language which they have, or are supposed to have (p. 484).—To an intelligent people it must appear utterly ridiculous that a prejudice is to be entertained against any Scotchman, without knowing who that Scotchman is, merely on account of his blood (p. 529).

In receiving a Gipsy, as a Gipsy, into society, there should be no kind of officious sympathy shown him, for he is too proud to submit to be made the object of it. Should he say that he is a Gipsy, the remark ought to be received as a mere matter of course, and little notice taken of it ; just as if it made no difference to the other party whether he was a Gipsy or not. A little surprise would be allowable ; but anything like condolence would be out of the question. And let the Gipsy himself, rather, talk upon the subject, than a desire be shown to ask him questions, unless his remarks should allow them, in a natural way, to be put to him. . . . . Such an admission on the part of a Gipsy would presumptively prove that he was a really candid and upright person ; for few Scottish Gipsies, beyond those about Yetholm, would make such a confession (p. 445).—In approaching one of this class we should be careful not to express that prejudice for him as a Gipsy which we might have for him as a man ; for it is natural enough to feel a dislike for many people whom we meet with, and which, if the people were Gipsies, we might insensibly allow to fall upon them on account of tribe alone ; so difficult is it to shake one's self clear of the prejudice of caste towards the Gipsy name (p. 483).—It is no business of mine to ask them, how long it is since their ancestors left the tent, or, indeed, if they even know when that occurred ; and still less, if they know when any of them ever did anything that was contrary to law. Still, one feels a little irksome in such a Gipsy's company, until the Gipsy question has been fairly brought before the world, and the point settled, that a Gipsy may be a gentleman, and that no disparagement is necessarily connected with the name, considered in itself. . . . . Let the name of Gipsy be as much respected, in Scotland, as it is now de-spised, and the community would stare to see the civilized Gipsies make their appearance ; they would come buzzing out, like bees, emerging even from places where a person, not in the secret, never would have dreamt of (p. 481).—The fact of these Gipsies being received into society, and respected as Gipsies (as it is with them at present as men), could not fail to have a wonderful effect upon many of the humble, ignorant, or wild ones. They would perceive, at once, that the objections which the community had to them proceeded, not from their being Gipsies, but from their habits only (p. 436).

Speaking of part of the race who live like other people, I have said that "one feels a little irksome in such a Gipsy's company"; which is illustrated by the following circumstance. A little before the publication of the *History of the Gipsies*, I accidentally mentioned my intention to a Scotchman, living in New York, with whom I dealt for articles of personal use, when he dropped a remark that led me instantly to discontinue the subject, and try him the next time I called on him. I then entered fully into it, as indirectly applicable to himself, when he brought his hand down on his counter with an oath, and said, " I am one myself, for ours is a Gipsy family." The only remark I made in reply was, that "there are plenty of them." This man looked like an ordinary Scotchman, but was far above the average of his class, and much respected, and worthy of respect. The next time we met, his eyes did not catch mine, nor mine his, and we never again alluded to the Gipsies in any way. As a means of giving an idea of what is perhaps too abstract for some people easily to understand, his confession might be used as a catch-phrase, to illustrate a Gipsy of a certain kind— " I am one myself, for ours is a Gipsy family"; that is, one of this eastern race that arrived so recently in Scotland, while following a tented life, and whose descendants, owing to a mixture of native blood, are now to be found of all colours.

Lightning Source UK Ltd.
Milton Keynes UK
UKHW020157271020
372285UK00005B/596